"THE CHILDREN OF JEWISH—GENTILE INTERMARRIAGE LIVE IN TWO WORLDS."

We are born into two cultures, and spend the rest of our lives traveling back and forth between them. Most of us eventually settle in a primary religious-ethnic "country of residence," but choosing it is a lengthy and complex process. This book explores that process. It also serves as a practical guide for descendants of intermarriage (and other persons in their lives) who seek happy and positive resolutions to dilemmas that grow more common each year as the intermarriage rate rises.

Given that our duality affects our lives in such intimate and even dramatic ways, it is important that adult children of intermarriage, their families, and the Jewish and Christian communities recognize the permanent cultural balancing act that each of us must perform.

And most importantly, we and those dear to us need information about how other children of intermarriage have dealt with their identity dilemmas. Such knowledge not only eases our own teenage and adult identity struggles, but shows us that we are not abnormal, or alone in our difficulties. We are simply experiencing the same problems facing other children of intermarriage, and like them, we can find honorable, psychologically healthy solutions.

BETWEEN TWO WORLDS:

*Choices for Grown Children
of Jewish-Christian Parents*

Leslie Goodman-Malamuth
and
Robin Margolis

POCKET BOOKS

New York   London   Toronto   Sydney   Tokyo   Singapore

An *Original* publication of POCKET BOOKS

POCKET BOOKS, a division of Simon & Schuster Inc.
1230 Avenue of the Americas, New York, NY 10020

Goodman-Malamuth, Leslie.
   Between two worlds : choices for grown children of Jewish-
Christian parents / Leslie Goodman-Malamuth and Robin Margolis.
      p. cm.
   Includes bibliographical references.
   ISBN: 0-671-70007-3 : $10.00
   1. Interfaith marriage—United States. 2. Interfaith families—
United States. 3. Children of interfaith marriage—United States.
4. Jews—United States—Families—Religious life. 5. Group
identity—United States. 6. Identity (Psychology)—United States.
I. Margolis, Robin. II. Title.
HQ1031.G58   1992
306.84'3—dc20   91-22930
                                                                          CIP

First Pocket Books trade paperback printing January 1992

10 9 8 7 6 5 4 3 2 1

POCKET and colophon are registered trademarks of
Simon & Schuster Inc.

Printed in the U.S.A.

   We gratefully acknowledge permission to reprint from the following materials:
   Stage V: A Journey Through Illness, by Sonny Wainwright. Berkeley, California: Acacia
Books, 1984, pp. 69–70. Reprinted by permission of Joan Nestle.
   " 'Hebrew-Christians': Who Are They?," by Rabbi Michael Skobac. Baltimore, Mary-
land: *Jews for Judaism Newsletter*, August 1990, pp. 2–3.
   You Might As Well Live: The Life and Times of Dorothy Parker, by John Keats. New York:
Bantam Books, 1972, p. 156. Reprinted by permission of Sterling Lord Literistic, Inc.
Copyright 1972 by John Keats.
   An Alchemy of Genres: Cross-Genre Writings by American Women Poet-Critics, by Diane
P. Freedman. Charlottesville, Virginia: University Press of Virginia, to be published in
1992.
   Lovesong: Becoming a Jew, by Julius Lester. New York: Henry Holt & Co., 1988,
p. 11.
   "What Color Is Jesus?: When Your Mother Is White and Your Father Is Black, The
Questions Never Stop," by James McBride. *Washington Post Magazine*, July 31, 1988,
p. 26.
   "Rabbis Can Help By Speaking Out" [Against Sexual Abuse in Jewish Families], by
Rabbi Irving Greenberg. *Moment*, April 1990, p. 49.
   Margaret Bourke-White: A Biography, by Vicki Goldberg. Copyright © 1986. New York:
HarperCollins Publishers, 1986, pp. 4–5, 41, and 43.

To our beloved grandmothers
Mae Goodman-Malamuth (1894–1991)
and Marie Margolis Miles (1900–1991)

*May the memory of the righteous
endure as a blessing*

Acknowledgments

Our profoundest gratitude goes to the hundreds of adult children and grandchildren of Jewish-Gentile intermarriage who shared their lives with us. Without their honesty, indignation, humor, clarity, confusion, pain, and uplift, there would be no book. We also appreciate everyone—too numerous to name individually—in the Jewish, Christian, and secular communities who championed our pet subject and encouraged us to continue. Thank you to B'nai B'rith Women International, the Jewish Study Center of Washington, D.C., the Rabbinical Assembly, and the synagogues, *havurot*, and Hadassah and ORT chapters that invited us to speak, as well as the print, television, and radio journalists who solicited our opinions. It is heartening to see these groups and individuals take the descendants of intermarriage as seriously as we need to be taken.

Joan Mizrahi really should be considered the third author of this book, as she's been an integral and cherished participant from its earliest days. Lee Gruzen has long been our sounding board and backstop—thank you, Lee, for your love and support. Bruce Maliken's computer software and expertise took our mailing list off its dog-eared sheets of Avery labels and into the twentieth century. We thank Diane Freedman, Eric Fusfield, Susan LaDuca, Karen Solomon, and Stephen "This Old Heart of Mine" Weiner for allowing us to read their published and unpublished writings. Our tireless agent, Agnes Birnbaum, never lost faith even when ours faltered, and deserves much of the credit for our perseverance. The invaluable suggestions of Leslie Wells, our editor at Pocket Books, and Ellen Cowhey's deft line editing lent substance and style to the book. Thank you, Denise Silvestro, for guiding us through the last steps before publication.

Leslie's life would scarcely be worth living without Jeanette Morrison, the best correspondent and friend that any shut-in could wish for. Thanks, too, to everyone else who's boosted her spirits as this book took shape, including Neil Carter, Barbara Grogan Costelloe, Paula Desio, Harriet Ed-

Ackowledgments

wards, Luz Figueroa, Ruth Kincaid, Wilhelmina Larbi, Jan Leonard, Mary Alice Levine, Stacey Levy, Philip Malamuth, Sherry Maliken, Kim Masters, Rachel Metrikin-Gold, June Nelson, Geoff Piker, Chuck Shepherd, Eleanor Smith, William F. Thompson, M.D., Bill Weiswasser, Sarah Weldon, the Mothers' Small Group of Washington Independent Writers, Lise Antinozzi and the gang from Washington Grocery Service, and the families of the North Cleveland Park Babysitting Co-op. Barry David Nelson was born soon after Pocket Books bought the proposal for this book and has known no other mother than the one who "works for the kangaroo," as his big brother Gabriel puts it. Steve Nelson deserves the Nobel Peace Prize for his patience, generosity, and good-natured acceptance of chaos. Steve's the straw that stirs the drink.

Robin thanks James LeBron Mosley, Paula Danko, Jackie Lichtman-Linden, and Ruth Berman for their longstanding friendship and encouragement. Margo, Lynn, Mary Catherine, and Peg also cheered Robin on through the years it took to become a "real" writer. She appreciates the professional assistance she received from Isolde Chapin of Washington Independent Writers, Hannelore Hahn of the International Women's Writing Guild, and Jamie Heller. Special thanks are owed to Victoria Diaz, M.D., Mindy Jacobs, Ph.D., Allen Mondzac, M.D., L. Carole Richardson, D.D.S., and Shawna Willey, M.D., who helped heal Robin in body and soul when she was diagnosed with breast cancer three months after signing the contract for this book. Robin is very grateful to her long-suffering father, Frederic N. Smith, for his unstinting emotional and financial support. And Robin's debt to her late mother, Phyllis Miles Smith, whose life and death started the journey that led to this book, is complex, karmic, and deeply felt.

Contents

ix

Contents

x

BETWEEN
TWO
WORLDS

My Mother's Funeral Papers

LESLIE GOODMAN-MALAMUTH AND I EACH HAVE ONE JEWISH and one Gentile parent. Most descendants of intermarriage are aware of their status from a very early age, as Leslie was. But some of us don't discover our dual heritage until we are adults. Perhaps one day the telephone rings, and at the other end of the line is a relative we never knew existed. Or we might find a *siddur* (Jewish prayer book), its leather covers limp with age and handling, tucked behind our father's books. If our hand closes around a rosary in our mother's sewing box, instead of the tape measure we're looking for, Mom may redden guiltily and admit that it is hers. We then learn for the first time that we belong in two worlds.

One November day in 1984, my life changed forever. Six weeks had passed since my mother's death. I reluctantly returned to my parents' home, which I had visited only once in the preceding four years, on the day of my mother's funeral. My father had asked me to clean out my mother's closet and bureau for him, and though I'd agreed to, inwardly I resisted the task. It seemed uncomfortably personal to paw through her possessions, now that she couldn't defend them from me.

When I was a child, my mother and I had loved each other deeply, but her growing depressions and irrational fits of rage had destroyed our relationship. By the time her cancer

1

took its final, fatal turn, we no longer met or telephoned.

I sometimes wondered idly if I was really her daughter, we were so unalike. She was, she said, of English and French-Canadian descent, and had raised me according to rigid Episcopalian and Republican principles. In appearance as well as demeanor, my mother and I were as different as the moon and the sun. My mother was short and dark. She resembled Claudette Colbert, and, like her screen sister, she always appeared in public perfectly groomed, favoring elegant suits and careful makeup. I am a female version of my WASP father, a retired naval officer; tall and thin, with his family's straight brown hair, blue eyes, long bony face, and fair skin that will not tan. I usually dressed in pullover sweaters and baggy jeans. People were always surprised to learn that we were mother and daughter.

Although I had stayed away from my parents' house for four years, I didn't feel I'd been gone that long. I had visited it plenty of times in my nightmares. In those dreams, my carefully constructed adult life vanished, and once again I was a teenager, burdened with three younger brothers and enduring my mother's bleak moods and terrifying rages. She acted as if she had a crime on her conscience, I sometimes thought, and then dismissed the idea as preposterous. What crime could a respectable military wife possibly have committed?

When I entered my parents' bedroom, I was alone in the house. I felt uneasy, like a burglar. I did not want to sift through my mother's possessions. She'd always been secretive, and fiercely protective of her belongings.

I unzipped my mother's garment bag and took out her formal gowns. She had been so beautiful. In my photo album, one snapshot showed her standing by my father, all dolled up, her face alight with joy, just before they left for a formal dinner at the Nixon White House.

At the bottom of the bag was a brown file pocket, which

2

I thought probably contained silk stockings; she had always carefully protected her expensive accessories. I untied the folder and pulled out a wedding license. In 1925, someone named Marie Levine had married a Bertram H. Margolis in New York City.

I was puzzled. I knew that my mother had put her parents in a nursing home six months before she died. Perhaps she had found this license in their house. But why would her parents keep someone else's personal papers?

An insurance policy from the early 1950s, confirming a name change. Marie Margolis had become Marie Miles. Miles? That was my mother's maiden name.

A birth certificate. A live white baby, Hyman Margolis, born to Daniel and Motie Margolis in a small town in upstate New York in 1901. Daniel was described as a street peddler. Both he and Motie had been born in Russia. The child had been delivered by a surgeon named Jacob J. Wolf. Jews, I thought. My mother's father was named Bertram H. Miles. Hyman Margolis?

The rest of the documents were tantalizingly incomplete. There was an empty envelope addressed to Marie Levine, bearing a Canadian postmark. Marie Levine's diplomas from a Canadian high school and teachers' college. A letter from a Canadian school board, noting that Sally Levine had confirmed Marie's birthdate. Bits and pieces, I thought, but enough that I could find these people, if they were still alive.

My mother was a Jew. Then I'm a Jew. A Jew!

There was a humming in my ears, and my mother's face floated before my eyes. That curly black hair, olive skin, huge brown eyes—a Jew! How could I not have known? One incident after another from my life crowded into my mind.

I am ten years old, alone with my mother one afternoon. "Are you trying to convert me, Robin?" she asks condescendingly. "I have my own form of religion. You practice religion your way, and I'll practice it my way." She walks off, leaving me to wonder why she has rejected my Sunday-school pamphlets.

I am twelve years old. I see my mother's parents. On the rare occasions that we visit them, they seem glad to see us, but nevertheless they appear nervous and fearful. I am never left alone with them for long. They have aquiline noses and broad New York accents. My mother has told us that they are Christians but indifferent to religion. My brothers and I enjoy their company because they indulgently let us explore all the books and objects in their home. My mother quarrels with them on this visit, and I do not see them again for fourteen years. Now I know that they are Jews. Why did they agree to keep my mother's secret?

I am seventeen years old. I am about to leave for college. My mother pulls me aside to tell me that if I ever decide to marry a Jew, she and my father will put no obstacles in my way. I cannot imagine why she has said this. Given the conservative southern school that I'll be attending, it's unlikely that I will ever even meet any Jews. Her voice dropping to a whisper, my mother says that Jewish men make good husbands. They don't drink or run around, she says, and they always bring their paychecks home.

I am twenty-six years old. My younger brother Andrew begins telling anti-Semitic jokes at lunch, one after another. My father is merely irritated at Andrew's adolescent vulgarity, but my mother is strangely silent and fearful. I order Andrew to shut up, and he does. My mother thanks me, her voice trembling. I am confused, for she is the tyrant of our house. If she wanted to silence Andrew, he would not dare to speak.

My mother was a Jew. I wondered how my father and brothers would greet this discovery. For years I had endured my black-sheep status as the family pauper, the writer, the women's libber, the bleeding-heart liberal, the agnostic, the

Democrat. Not an Episcopalian. Not a lady. Not the right stuff. Another wave of emotion overtook me—a desire for revenge, this time. How would my staunchly Christian brothers like to be half-Jews?

As my anger ebbed, a savage grief took its place. I stared at my parents' bed, in which my mother's life had gradually slipped away during the past few months. "Mother!" I shouted. "Mother! Why? Why did you do it?" I cried hysterically, gripping the footboard of the bed. There was no answer.

Exhausted, I yearned for comfort. I had an odd impulse to pray, but I was not sure why. As a child and a teenager, I had prayed often, in church and at home, only to be met by a blank wall of silence. At eighteen, I decided that religion was an irrational delusion and abandoned it. Several years later, I failed to pursue a passing interest in converting to Judaism, born as it was of a weak desire to reconnect myself somehow to a God whose existence I doubted.

Nevertheless, at that moment, I decided to pray. It couldn't hurt, I told myself. I did not clasp my hands or close my eyes. I gazed out my mother's bedroom window, looking at the golden afternoon sunlight slanting across the fading lawns and fields, and said that I was willing to live as a Jew. But what exactly did Jews do? I knew almost nothing about Judaism. I searched my memory.

"God," I said, "if You exist, I will live as a Jew. I'll take a Jewish last name. I'll join a synagogue." I paused in thought. Aha! "I'll send money to Israel. I'll learn Hebrew." I stopped. There had to be something more. I knew that when people became Christians, they offered their bodies and souls to the Lord Jesus Christ. What I had promised God didn't sound like enough. "I'll find my mother's relatives and learn why she did this," I added.

And then I was answered. It was not a vision or a voice. It was the feeling that comes when you telephone someone

5

you love, and there's that second of silence before he or she begins to speak. When I had prayed as a Christian, always I had experienced only the sound of a phone ringing, un-answered. But someone was listening this time. Someone who agreed to the bargain, and wanted me as a Jew.

I did not know it then, but I had begun a long psychic journey. I was to learn that just as my mother's world had reached out to claim me, so my father's world would not release me. I would learn that I must either find ways to live within both worlds or lose myself entirely.

CHAPTER

1

Who Are the Descendants of Intermarriage? Who Can Use This Book?

I feel Gentile in a synagogue and Jewish in a church.
—JEANNE,* THERAPIST

Since I have a background which includes more than one religion, I feel that I can be more open-minded with different religious institutions. . . . I feel very lucky to have a background which includes both Jewish and Quaker people.
—ROSS, CONSULTANT

When I was a child, I always asked new acquaintances about their religions, and when asked about mine, I would reply that I was half-Protestant and half-Jewish. In a way, this fact rather pleased me: It made me feel different and special. It also made me a perpetual doubter, from a very early age.
—NANCY, TEACHER

ONE AFTERNOON SEVERAL YEARS AGO, AS I WAS DOODLING ON my desk blotter, Robin telephoned. I was then a newspaper editor, and Robin and I frequently spoke about the freelance articles that she wrote for me. But as soon as I heard her voice that day, heavy with sorrow, I knew that this conversation would be different.

Robin blurted out the entire story of her mother's life and

---

* Jeanne is a real person. When only a first name is given (except for the authors'), a pseudonym has been used in order to protect the individual's anonymity.

deception, ending soberly, "I don't know anyone else who's the child of an intermarriage."

"You know *me*," I replied. And we began to discuss the subject, and we haven't stopped since.

Unlike Robin's, my story is undramatic. I now know that it is a fairly common one, too. My father, exposed to Christian Science in his childhood, has a secular, ethnic Jewish background, while my mother, who comes from a Protestant family, has never expressed a preference for any religious faith. I grew up in a determinedly secular home, with Christmas trees and Easter baskets, yet I was well into my teens before I learned what Easter was meant to signify.

Although strongly drawn to Judaism, I knew that *halacha* (Jewish law) defined only the children of Jewish mothers as Jews. So I laughingly referred to myself as "55 percent Jewish." From an early age, I had read everything I could find about Judaism. When I left home, at age seventeen, I observed the holidays as best I could, took courses in Jewish history and Hebrew, and crammed myself with information, as I would for an exam, about Jewish customs. I was married—by a priest—to a Catholic classmate from college and divorced him three years later. I was married—by a rabbi—to a Jewish colleague from the newspaper I worked for, and subsequently converted to Judaism, bore two sons, and gave them Hebrew names and a Jewish home environment. It was between my divorce and remarriage that I met Robin.

Exploring our status as children of intermarriage initially drew us together as friends, but we found that we had other things in common. We were both in our thirties, both journalists. Each of us had a Hoosier parent whose forebears had fought on the Union side in the Civil War. Our Jewish families were descended from Russian and Polish ancestors who had immigrated to the United States at the beginning of this century.

Whereas I'd had many years to attempt to come to terms

8

with my status as a child of intermarriage, Robin was still reeling from her discovery. She asked dozens of questions. Were there any books about people like us? (No? Why not?) Why hadn't any synagogues or churches started support groups? Was there a national organization addressing our concerns? Why did Jewish groups tend to squirm with discomfort at the mere existence of adult children of intermarriage? Why did well-intentioned synagogues offer us books and classes intended for interfaith couples when their concerns differed so markedly from ours? Why did Christian groups appear to take no interest in us at all?

Eventually, Robin and I decided we'd have to write the book and start the national organization ourselves. Through Pareveh, the Alliance for Adult Children of Jewish-Gentile Intermarriage, which we founded in 1985, we encountered hundreds of people who shared their stories with us in person, on the telephone, and through the mail. We amassed reams of material about descendants of intermarriage, both famous and obscure, whose lives have been documented in history and literature, from biblical narratives to supermarket tabloids. We discovered that people like us are everywhere, from California to Connecticut, New South Wales to Nova Scotia, and that we harbor many questions that have remained largely unacknowledged by our birth cultures.

Seeking still more information to give us a statistical base for this book, we sent lengthy questionnaires to the people on our mailing list whom we knew to be adult children or grandchildren of Jewish-Gentile intermarriage, and to other descendants who responded to authors' queries published in the book-review sections of *The New York Times*, *Washington Post*, and *Los Angeles Times*. An overwhelming 56 percent of those we contacted completed our questionnaire. These 185 respondents range in age from seventeen to seventy-eight, spanning several generations of child rearing by interfaith parents. They are also a geographically diverse group, spread throughout the United States, Canada, and several other countries.

Between Two Worlds is the first book to examine the personal and communal needs of the adult children and grandchildren of intermarriage from our *own* perspective. This book is for ourselves and for the friends, spouses, parents, grandparents, and others who care about us. *Between Two Worlds* is for people who work professionally with interfaith families, such as rabbis, priests, ministers, Jewish and Christian community group leaders, social workers, teachers, and psychologists. This book is for Jewish-Gentile couples raising their own little descendants of intermarriage, who by their sheer numbers have plenty of company these days but few positive role models and fewer eyewitness reports from interfaith marriages of the past. This book is also for readers who belong to none of the previous categories, those interested observers who remember only the scandal of the O'Reilly-Goldberg nuptials and never found out what happened after that.

However we ultimately choose to identify, we children of intermarriage are born into two worlds. As living links between two cultures, we spend our lives traveling back and forth between them, in ways that are obvious or subtle. Many of us eventually choose a primary "country of residence," but often only after a lengthy and complex internal struggle. And we can never completely sever all ties with our other, secondary culture. Through both positive and negative examples, *Between Two Worlds* demonstrates how the adult children and grandchildren of Jewish-Gentile intermarriage have learned to live with the permanent duality that is our birthright.

"I sometimes feel as though William Butler Yeats and Woody Allen are battling over my soul," jokes Patrick, who is Irish Catholic on his mother's side, Russian Jewish on his father's. Our mixed status has given us a rare sense of humor. Descendants of intermarriage, we find, are almost always quick to provide a quip that sums up how we perceive our situation. But once we stop laughing, a much more difficult task faces us: deciding how to balance our dual loyalties in order to live honorable and satisfying lives.

Our families complicate our choices, since neither they nor our two cultures can decide who "owns" our primary allegiance or how they can most effectively lobby to capture our loyalties. This issue is felt most acutely by the Jewish community, where a storm of controversy now swirls around the question, "Who is a Jew?", as it applies to the descendants of intermarriage (which we will discuss at greater length in chapter 3).

Jewish definitions of our status are contradicted, in turn, by Christian and Islamic laws. Christians claim any descendant of intermarriage who has been baptized, without regard for the status of their Jewish parent or grandparent. Islam's law of *Shari'ah* maintains that *all* children of Moslem fathers are Moslem. The status of the descendants of intermarriage is governed by secular definitions as well, such as Russia's internal passport regulations that define as Jews all persons of partly Jewish descent.

Disagreement among our parental cultures about our status has an immense emotional impact on us. After all, if our "two worlds" cannot agree on where we ultimately belong, or whether we can be—or should be—Jews or Christians or Moslems or whatever, we are left to resolve our duality as best we can. Being forced to do this, and to explain our choices to others, can be an irritating and exhausting task. "I came to resent others' need to identify me with one or the other," remarks Dana, who has a stereotypical Jewish surname yet considers herself neither Jewish nor Christian.

Seeking support from even our closest relatives and friends, we may come up empty-handed. People who come from homes in which both parents share a common faith and ethnicity often have real difficulty understanding how our loyalties may be divided two ways, three ways, or even more. Sophia, the daughter of a Greek Orthodox mother and a Jewish father, notes, "I've never fully felt I belonged to either group, yet I identify with both. When I was small, we lived nowhere near a Greek Orthodox church. My mother believed she'd be sinning not to give me a religious upbringing, so she sent me to a *Lutheran* Sunday school. She never even considered raising me Jewish." Is it any wonder that some of us are more than a little confused about where we belong—if anywhere?

Especially during the early years of our lives, our psychic passports clearly reveal our dual citizenship. We must explain ourselves, or be explained, at every major checkpoint of life, such as baptism, *bris* (ritual circumcision), or baby naming; confirmation, *bar* or *bat mitzvah;* meeting prospective in-laws; and while preparing for our weddings. Our children are born, with status problems of their own to resolve. We die, but on which side of the cemetery will we be laid to rest? (This last issue is more than a metaphor, as some Jewish cemeteries will not permit the interment of someone who was not, by their reckoning, a "real" Jew.)

"I do not like people to make assumptions about me based on my Semitic last name or appearance," complains Emma, who grew up nominally Christian "because it was the prevailing culture." Yet, the children of intermarriage often prompt lightning-fast assessments from people who wish to size us up quickly—and don't expect to find Nordic features, framed by flaxen hair, on someone named Rabinowitz.

Seemingly ordinary acts may prompt derision ("If you're Jewish, why are you sending Christmas presents to your brothers?") from those who don't understand our split allegiances. More ominously, our dual identities may subject us to tactless comments ("Since you're a Christian, do you agree with Louis Farrakhan when he says that Judaism is a 'gutter religion'?"), or it may even endanger our lives, as the Holocaust so horrifyingly demonstrated. For a number of descendants of Jewish-Gentile intermarriage, publicly identifying as Christians provided no protection whatsoever from annihilation.

Nowhere is our duality more apparent than in our relationships with our parents, also known as that sociological abstraction, "the interfaith couple." Whether our parents try to raise us in one culture, two cultures, a third culture, or none at all, we inevitably reflect both heritages, as surely as we have inherited one parent's perfect teeth and the other's flat feet. And if well-meaning parents say that we may choose our primary identity when we grow up, such freedom might actually tie our hands. A number of descendants of intermarriage say they are reluctant to favor one culture—one parent!—over another, as Angela confirms. Although her Italian-Catholic father and Jewish mother left the decision up to her, Angela reports that she still feels paralyzed.

> I tell you, I feel like a traitor. If I go to a synagogue, I'm betraying my father. If I go to church, I think how my mother would object. I feel like I can't go to either one!

As the children of interfaith couples mature, the parents learn that there are no guarantees about our future religious or ethnic identities, no matter how they raise us. Some believe that if one partner converts to the other's faith in the name of family unity and "for the children's sake," their offspring will not be affected by their dual heritages. Not so, say our interviewees. Elliott remarks that as a child he was always aware that his mother, converted under Orthodox Jewish auspices, had been born Gentile.

> No one in our Jewish neighborhood thought she was a Jew. She didn't talk like a Jew, she didn't look like a Jew.

One day my sister came home from [Reform Jewish] Sunday school crying, and said, "We're not Jews, because our mother isn't a Jew." My father got angry and said, "She converted, she's a Jew! I don't want to hear any more about it!"

Despite his upbringing in a Jewish home, Elliott says that he has never felt like a "real" Jew. Now in his forties, Elliott recently married for the first time; like his father, he chose a Gentile wife.

So deep is our duality, and so tightly are we tied to both parents, that even when divorce, death, abuse, adoption, or illness separates us from our mothers or fathers, their heritage leaves a strong imprint upon us, even if we are not fully aware of our dual backgrounds or the circumstances of our births. If descendants of intermarriage make a discovery as remarkable as Avram's, our lives may change accordingly, as we seek fully to experience our missing "half."

"I always knew I was adopted—no problem there," says Avram, a graduate student in his midtwenties. "And, when I entered college, I intended to become a Protestant minister." Seeking more information about his biological parents, at age twenty-one he went to the agency that had matched him with his adoptive mother. "It was a *Jewish* agency!" he exclaims, adding:

I asked, "Hey, what's going on here?" They showed me some papers, and I learned that my birth mother was a Jew, though my father wasn't. She was young and unmarried, so she put me up for adoption. It was like an electrical shock. I immediately decided that I wasn't going to be a pastor after all, and started going to an Orthodox *shul*. . . .

My [adoptive] mother can't talk about this with me at all. I'd like to find my Jewish mother someday.

14

Like most children of interfaith relationships, Avram found that he couldn't just leave one world without a backward glance to settle wholly within his other culture. He continues to live with and care for his elderly, ailing Christian adoptive mother, but he keeps kosher, observes the Jewish holidays, and covers his head with a *kipah* (skullcap).

Grandchildren, great-grandchildren, and even great-great-grandchildren of Jewish-Gentile intermarriage have reported identity conflicts similar to those of the adult children. Twentysomething Peggy was happily planning her wedding when her father dropped the bombshell.

I grew up in the Midwest, in a Jewish home. I had always thought my [paternal] grandmother was a German Jew, but then not long ago Dad told me that she was a Christian. I know I'm supposed to be Jewish because my mother is a Jew, but I feel horribly betrayed, because I truly adored my grandmother, and she lied to me. She knew all of the Jewish things—food, ceremonies—but she never converted. She was pretending for my [Jewish] grandfather's sake. He didn't want it known that he had married a Christian.

I have to wonder, now, am I a real Jew? I mean, one-fourth of me is Christian!

Even if solidly ensconced in the Jewish or the Christian community, virtually all the descendants of intermarriage we've spoken to say that they're keenly aware of their other heritage, however fractional that kinship may appear to others. Perhaps the most heroic example of how such a dual allegiance can be lived out is that of Raoul Wallenberg.

A Swedish Lutheran, raised in a wealthy, well-connected family, Wallenberg appeared to be a thoroughly assimilated Christian descendant of intermarriage. Yet, Wallenberg, who became a partner in a Jewish-owned trading firm, was intensely proud of his Jewish great-great-grandfather who had died many years before he was born. As a young man, Raoul boasted to a friend, "Someone like me, who is both a Jew and a Wallenberg, can never be defeated."

When the Third Reich's "Final Solution" began, Wallenberg volunteered for a diplomatic post in Hungary. There, he was able to issue Swedish passports to many Jews, thus sparing them one-way trips to the Nazi death camps. He was finally captured by the Russians and vanished into the Soviet prison system. He paid with his life for his tie to the Jewish people.

Since our duality affects our lives in such intimate and even dramatic ways, it is important that interfaith parents, grandparents, and other family members recognize the permanent cultural balancing act that each descendant must perform. We need to share information about how others in our situation have dealt with their identity dilemmas. Such knowledge not only eases our lifelong quest for a harmoniously balanced identity, but shows us that we are not abnormal or alone in our difficulties. We are simply experiencing the same problems facing other descendants of intermarriage, and, like them, we can find our way safely home.

Virtually all of the hundreds of adult children and grandchildren of intermarriage we've spoken to report *some* difficulty *somewhere* in balancing the two worlds from which we come. In some cases, the conflicts are quite easily resolved, and the descendants' lives are delightfully enhanced in the process. "I don't see my status as a child of intermarriage as a problem. I relish it. It gives me freedom. It provides shock value when I'm in the mood to poke at a dogmatic jerk," says Kris, the daughter of a Jewish woman and Protestant man.

Hans, a retired diplomat, remarks that his blended heritage has left him "wary of dogma and sectarian certainties.

All my past experience contributes to my present self. Labels are not a significant factor in my Unitarian synthesis. I don't live between two worlds. I live in one, full of variety and stimulation." His sunny, secure attitude is shared by Kevin, who says, "Both of my heritages have good values. Judaism tempers me with humanism and places the correct values on family and education. Episcopalians have grace under pressure and understand the pursuit of a life of serenity."

These souls radiate psychological robustness, and we're glad of it. But others have told us that living with a split heritage remains deeply troubling and is never far from their minds. Even choosing to lead a wholly secular life, without identifying as a Jew or as a Christian, appears to be a more highly charged issue for the adult children of intermarriage than for our friends who were raised in homes in which a single faith and ethnicity prevailed. In the course of our research, we've noted that one of the biggest differences between these two groups is that secular individuals from endogamous homes tend to be genuinely low-key about their lack of affiliation, which they usually can explain with a certain measure of detachment.

Conversely, scratch a secular adult child or grandchild of intermarriage, and you may be overwhelmed by the gush of long-suppressed feelings. For descendants who have difficulty handling the unavoidable, seesawing pull between our "two halves," the choice to live a secular life is often conceived in pain rather than in a lack of interest in a religiously observant life, as it might be for a "born" Jew or Christian.

In our experience, adult children and grandchildren of intermarriage appear to be much more emotionally attracted to or revolted by religious institutions than people who have two Jewish or two Christian parents. Even if they view the religious culture of their childhood with distaste or disinterest, "all-Jewish" or "all-Christian" individuals know that it will always be there for them if they choose to return to it. Whether we lead secular or religious lives, the adult children of intermarriage do not enjoy that kind of assurance, as our status is not nearly as clear-cut.

Our problems in adjusting to our duality have implications beyond ourselves and our families and friends. Both of our worlds need us. For those of us who choose to live as Christians, learning to love and cherish our Jewish "half" can only help foster cordial Jewish-Christian relations, while working to vanquish anti-Semitism. And those of us who decide to live as Jews will determine whether many Jewish communities outside of Israel will survive.

Millions of descendants of Jewish-Gentile intermarriage live in Jewish communities and other cultures all over the world. No one knows precisely how many of us there are. Estimates of our numbers in the United States alone range from half a million to a million or more. Although estimates of today's intermarriage rate vary, the American Jewish Committee reckons that the out-marriage rate for Jews in this country remained under 10 percent prior to 1960, rose to 17.4 percent between 1961 and 1965, ballooned to 31.7 percent by 1972, currently runs 33 to 40 percent nationwide— and is expected to reach 50 percent by the year 2000. In countries as disparate as the United States and Peru, intermarriage rates between Jews and Christians are so high that by the year 2030, it is likely that the offspring of those marriages will outnumber Jews who have two Jewish parents.

Consequently, the descendants of Jewish-Christian intermarriage hold the swing vote in determining the future of Diaspora Judaism. Our allegiance to the Jewish people has yet to be courted seriously. If the descendants of intermarriage largely opt not to identify as Jews, in the coming years Jewish communities outside of Israel will dwindle markedly, and many will disappear altogether.

While Jewish law forbids marriage between Jews and unconverted Gentiles, with so many Jews nonetheless choosing non-Jewish spouses, all sectors of Judaism must adopt a broad-based humane approach that will welcome interfaith families and their offspring into the Jewish community. Intermarriage between Jews and Christians is a fact of life that must be dealt with constructively, rather than be perceived as an irredeemable disaster for either Judaism or Christianity.

Those of us who choose to live as Jews will replenish Jewish communities worldwide, whose ranks are being depleted by assimilation and apathy. The importance to Judaism of Jewish outreach to interfaith families cannot be underestimated. Scores of children and grandchildren of intermarriage, whether the offspring of Jewish mothers or Jewish fathers, have told us that they were made to feel distinctly unwelcome by the Jewish establishment. Some weathered the disapproval and became active, committed Jews, while others slunk away, wistful, disappointed, and even bitter.

Christianity has some obligations in this area, too. Christian-identified descendants of intermarriage, although efficiently processed by Christianity's two-thousand-year history of welcoming and integrating newcomers, often find that their problems in dealing with their duality are not understood by their fellow Christians. Even amid institutional welcome, they may feel quite alone.

Our concerns about ethnicity, faith, and identity are—and must be—very different from those of our parents, the great majority of whom came of age in homes with two Jewish or two Christian parents. Although we applaud the effort that has gone into creating the new Jewish outreach efforts (and the rare Christian group) that target interfaith families, these groups erroneously consider our needs identical to those of our parents. Attempting to cover interfaith couples *and* their children with a single umbrella program—even with the best of intentions—means that the descendants of intermarriage are likely to be left out in the rain.

Not only must the Jewish and Christian communities recognize our unique needs, and develop programs to accommodate them, but we ourselves need to acknowledge and address the ways in which we differ from our interfaith parents. Accepting our duality is crucial to our healthy development, say descendants of intermarriage. Understanding our duality eases our journey to a settled adult identity, a voyage that permits few shortcuts.

CHAPTER
2

As Our Hybrid Seeds Begin to Grow— Childhood and Beyond

I went home from [Baptist] Sunday school one day and cried as I told my mother that the teacher had said that the Jews— which I took to include my Jewish father—were going to hell because they didn't believe in Jesus. [My mother] assured me that this was not true. The teacher later asked my mother if I were an atheist.

—ELOISE, RETIRED TEACHER

When I was nine, I was ready to go to a Jewish summer camp with all my friends. One week before I was to leave, the director of the camp called me and told me I couldn't go because my mother wasn't Jewish and therefore neither was I. She had no right to determine my identification!

—HANNAH, CLINICAL PSYCHOLOGIST

"LESLIE, CAN YOU HELP ME OUT?" MY FRIEND ELAINE PLEADED one day several years ago. "I'm not going to be able to teach that after-school cooking class at the Jewish Community Center after all. Could you? It's only once a week."

"Sure," I said. Even though I was heavily pregnant with my first child, I felt I was up to the task. And it *was* fun.

Eighteen rambunctious kids, five to seven years old, would burst through the door, and then the flour, eggshells, and measuring spoons flew around the room for an hour. I'd collapse in a corner as my sticky charges proudly carried the fruits of their labors—soft pretzels, pizza bagels, Sephardic *sambusak,* and chocolate-dipped *matzah*—home to their parents.

The kids didn't know that I hadn't started life as a "real" Jew, or that I savor the irony of pretending that I have spent my whole life feeling comfortable in Jewish settings. Like many other descendants of intermarriage, I've learned to "pass," and not to be discomfited when a six-year-old corrects my pronunciation ("It's *Pe-sachhhh,* Mrs. Nelson") or questions my certifiably Jewish husband's background ("Nelson isn't a Jewish name!").

One little girl liked to stay after class and talk to me. Just before Passover, Sheila drew a deep breath and confided, "Ummm, Mrs. Nelson? We're not going to have a *seder* [traditional Passover dinner]."

"Lots of people don't have a *seder,*" I said, wiping spattered egg yolk off the floor.

"Well, we don't have one because they make my mother nervous," she continued, stammering, "You see, my mother . . . my mother isn't Jewish."

I smoothed the hair off her forehead, which was furrowed with anxiety. "I'll tell you a little secret, Sheila," I said. "Neither is mine."

I knew how she felt. Years before, when I was small and anxious too, I'd felt that I wasn't quite like the other kids in my public elementary school, virtually all of whom were Gentiles. If my family shunned Christianity, if I bore the obviously Jewish surname of Goodman-Malamuth, as prominent as my thick glasses and orthopedic shoes, did that mean I was Jewish? I could see the wheels turning in Sheila's mind. If her parents had sent her to roll out bagel dough in a Jewish after-school program, did *that* mean she was Jewish?

Evidently, Sheila's parents had decided to raise her in only one culture—her father's. But perhaps they didn't realize that telling their child that she was a Jew and raising her in a "Jewish home" would not prevent her from seeing that one parent wasn't Jewish by birth. And it couldn't keep her from being touchingly sensitive to her mother's needs, while striving to meet her father's expectations for his "Jewish" child.

Nor had exposing her to Jewish observances shielded her from the sad awareness, at the tender age of six, that many other Jews—starting with her classmates—would view her as less than legitimate once they learned that her mother had been born Gentile. It's hard enough being a kid, but Sheila shoulders an additional burden: learning to live in two worlds.

Her situation cannot be considered unusual. Three-quarters of those we interviewed, both formally and informally, are the adult children or grandchildren of a Jewish man and a Gentile woman. Even halachically "correct," matrilineal descendants of intermarriage have related similar stories of insecurity and rejection as children in the Jewish and Christian communities. And since our parents come from two historically opposed religious and ethnic traditions, they transmit different messages to us when they provide the templates for our adult lives. We must draw what is appropriate for us from our clashing role models in order to create a single workable identity for ourselves.

Two parents, two messages. Isn't that the way all children learn to define themselves? Yes. But children of two ethnically Jewish parents rest secure in the knowledge that they themselves *are* Jews and that their family's Jewishness generally is not in question, even if their parents differ in their observance of Jewish traditions. The children of two born-Gentile, Christian parents benefit from the same security.

Although our interfaith parents may have demonstrated, as one questionnaire respondent pointed out, a strong desire "to assimilate and to lead lives not dominated by religion," we descendants of intermarriage live in ethnic and religious cultures that attempt to pigeonhole us, neatly and immediately. Not only do these worlds not recognize our duality, but they may go out of their way to avoiding dealing with it. "Society tends to dichotomize, and tries to define you. You're either one or the other, but never both. It's hard to integrate in the face of this pressure to define yourself," notes Stewart, the son of a Jewish father and an "atheist, Protestant-raised" mother.

Our search for ways to build stable religious and ethnic identities begins at the moment of our births. Many interfaith couples skip all ritual recognition of their new child, while others choose to initiate us immediately into one parental culture through baptism, *bris,* or Jewish baby naming. If our parents have agreed to continue practicing their own religions, and will be teaching both belief systems to us, chances are they already have begun a hidden tug-of-war for our allegiance, and the choice of a birth ceremony represents the opening salvo for one side. Perhaps our parents plan to introduce us to a religious culture that is equally foreign to both of them, which they hope will enable them to compromise the differences between their two cultures.

The presence or absence of our grandparents at a birth ceremony makes a statement of its own. Our grandparents are likely to be present if we are being initiated into their religious tradition. If not, they may boycott the ceremony. If our parents plan to raise us in a religious or ethnic culture that is not the same as our grandparents', they may show their distress by maintaining only perfunctory relationships with us, or by storming out of our lives altogether. A young Jewish couple reported to us that their great-aunt had told them that she plans to leave them all of her money, because her other relatives have married out of the faith. "Their children won't be 'real' Jews," the elderly woman lamented.

So loaded are the rituals of our early lives that some children of intermarriage are circumcised or baptized secretly, with no party or photographs—not unlike a shotgun wedding—in order to avoid agitating relatives. In some interfaith families, loyalties are so divided that their life-cycle choices differ from child to child. The eldest of four children, Andrea says that she was the only one of her parents' offspring to be baptized in her mother's "Ukrainian-style" Catholic faith. "But I was not told this—or that I had godparents—until I was about twelve," she notes.

Other interfaith couples are so desperate to please everyone that they attempt, as the Yiddish proverb goes, "to dance at two weddings with one *tuchus* [derriere]." These parents have told us that they plan to raise one child as a Jew, another as a Christian. Others ask if they should discreetly hold a *bris* for the benefit of the Jewish side of the family, then baptize the child at a separate function, without telling the *mohel* (ritual circumcisor), the priest, or the two rival camps that the other ceremony has taken place.

It would be easy, but unfair, to fault our parents for some of these early attempts to cope with our duality. Although weird family dynamics may result from trying to raise children in different faiths within the same household, or from simultaneously welcoming us into two vehemently opposed cultures, these efforts do represent an earnest attempt to recognize our duality, in however distorted a way.

There are four primary child-rearing options for interfaith parents:

- They may raise us in one culture, to which our other parent may or may not convert.
- They may raise us conscientiously in both cultures.
- They may select a third culture.
- They may raise us with no particular religious or cultural traditions at all.

Of the 185 individuals who responded to our questionnaire:

- Seventeen percent were raised as Jews.
- Forty-one percent were raised as Christians (including Unitarians and Quakers).
- Nineteen percent were raised with exposure—slight or significant—to both cultures.
- Twenty-three percent were raised in a third, "compromise" culture, or in no specific culture.

There's a lot riding on this decision. Since our parents usually have not themselves grown up in bicultural homes, many of their children's emotional needs remain a mystery to them. Yet, interfaith couples fervently hope that the option they select for their children will please them and satisfy everyone in their extended families. In addition, the couple would like to guarantee that as adults, their children will make spiritual and cultural choices of affiliation that will gratify *both* parents equally. As our interviewees have stated—often with passionate exasperation—achieving all of these worthy objectives is nearly impossible.

"The issue of conflicting loyalties will naturally arise, and some families will adapt well if they are healthy and flexible, while others will suffer if they are rigid and dysfunctional," says Marie, the daughter of a Jewish father and an atheist mother who was raised as a Protestant. Even though perfection is unattainable—just as it is for single-faith couples—interfaith parents can indeed nurture children who love and cherish both of their "halves." That's what happened in Helga's family. She and her brother and sister all brim over with affection and respect for their parents' earnest efforts to create a harmonious interfaith family environment, without denying that the family was "different." Says Helga:

My parents fell in love in spite of religious differences. They had over thirty years of happy marriage before my father's death. However, it was not always easy! My Jewish grandmother sat on Daddy's suitcase and refused to let him go away to marry Mama. He went anyhow. Grand-mother sat *shivah* [Jewish period of mourning], but even-tually she welcomed them back. I think Mama felt that her in-laws always blamed her for taking their son—the cho-sen!—away from the fold, though he never changed his faith.

My parents were engaged for five years, and they were married for four years before they started their family, because they didn't know how to solve the dilemma of how to raise us. They finally decided that our religious foundation would be determined by where they settled. If we were in New York City, we would be Jewish, and if we lived in the rural South, we would be raised as Christians.

Helga's family eventually moved to a southern state, where the children were indeed brought up as Christians. Helga and her siblings visited her father's family yearly, "but we never knew our Jewish relatives intimately when we were children." Yet, notes Helga, "There were never any secrets regarding either parent's faith. I'm proud of my status as a child of intermarriage, and of my wonderful parents, who did not let religious differences interfere with their great love and respect for each other." Today, Helga is married to an Episcopalian, but belongs "to no organized religious insti-tution or group."

Helga's parents' efforts appear even more admirable in light of the fact that they set up housekeeping more than fifty years ago, without enjoying the support of positive role models or guidance from the Jewish or the Christian com-munity. Things are better for interfaith couples today, but the process of dealing with the children's duality is often hastily glossed over or ignored by the small body of literature aimed at interfaith families.

When interfaith couples of today turn to the experts for suggestions on how to raise us, they encounter representatives of three rival schools of thought.

Raise 'em in one culture only. This camp argues that the children should be raised in only one culture, preferably Judaism. Those advocating this position place stringent and unambiguous demands upon interfaith couples. The children's non-Jewish parent should convert to Judaism, ideally before the wedding takes place. At the very least, they argue, the non-Jewish spouse must agree to raise the children as Jews, and maintain a wholly Jewish home, even if that spouse does not wish to convert. Ironically, this is exactly the position taken by Christianity about interfaith marriages for most of its two-thousand-year history: the Jewish spouse is often urged to convert and to promise to rear the offspring in a wholly Christian home.

Unlike the historical Christian position, which holds that children of intermarriage who are raised as Jews will not find salvation, the "raise 'em in one" proponents of Judaism don't argue that such children will get a better deal in the afterlife. Rather, they imply that if both Judaism and Christianity get equal emphasis in the interfaith home, the children will become confused, neurotic adults.

In order to spare these children the pain of choosing a heritage, the "raise 'em in one" advocates suggest that one parent should be designated the spiritual standard-bearer at the outset of the marriage. Of course, this means that a lower status is assigned to the parent whose religion is not observed in the home; one recent book on intermarriage termed this person the "out-parent." Among our respondents, patrilineals who were raised as "real" Jews appear particularly aware of how their born-Gentile mothers are pressured by the Jewish community to downplay their backgrounds and to instill Jewish values in their children.

There are both advantages and problems with the "raise 'em in one" approach. Fortunately, there are families like Helga's, in which the interfaith parents have successfully brought up children in one religion without becoming unduly uncomfortable with the background of the "out-parent." A home with one religious faith, but two *cultural* identities, can offer a richly nurturing environment for children. In Anita's case, such a home even provided distinct culinary advantages. She reminisces, "Mother always made chicken soup *and* black-eyed peas, blintzes *and* fruitcake—she was from Texas!"

Her father, a cattle dealer and farmer, "was raised as an Orthodox Jew, but he didn't care that much about his religion. My mother was Southern Baptist, and it was important to her to raise us with *something*," she says. Her mother's task was complicated by the fact that for much of her children's early years, the family lived in the rural Midwest, where there were "few or no other Jews," Anita notes, adding:

> When we moved to a town with a temple, Mother became active, and drove through snowstorms to get us to Sunday and Hebrew school. It was due to her that we all grew up with these positive feelings toward the Jewish religion.
>
> She converted to Judaism when I was twelve, and all four of us children accompanied her to the *mikveh* [ritual bath].

Families committed to raising children solely as Jews do not escape the so-called "December dilemma," which plagues all interfaith families, as Nora and many other respondents can attest. Her mother, a Methodist who converted to Judaism before marriage, "did more than anyone to instill a Jewish spirit in my brother and me," says Nora, adding:

My mother lit *Shabbos* candles every week for years, prepared *seders,* recited prayers. When, in a fit of teenage rebellion, I decided not to attend High Holy Day services, it was *she* who got upset with me. She would drive me and my brother around our area to admire the Christmas decorations, but we couldn't express regrets over not celebrating the holiday because "it'll upset your father," she'd say.

Many born-Gentiles married to Jews learn quickly to downplay any sentimental attachment they may have to non-Jewish holidays and rituals, but as Nora's mother demonstrates, their ties to them can never be fully severed. A Christmas tree, for example, becomes an especially potent image of what they may have left behind. The Christian symbolism that is present, however discreetly, in every interfaith family frequently gives the Jewish parent, as well as the Jewish community, the willies. It is easy for Jewish pundits to decree sternly that "real" Jews don't have Christmas trees, but since they can't rule against having an Aunt Mary Kate with her Mass cards and rosary beads, they simply try to ignore her existence. It's easier to focus Jewish anxiety on those twinkling, enticing Christmas trees.

The tree proscription may not be an issue for the rare interfaith home in which the non-Jewish partner doesn't mind giving short shrift to Christian holidays. But the no-tree edict causes endless trouble in the Jewish-identified interfaith family in which the Christian parent wants to preserve at least some vestige of his or her birth culture. Does such a family, raising their children as Jews, ban the tree on home turf but permit the kids to carouse around it at an uncle's house? What difference will it ultimately make to the family's identity where the tree is? What if the Jewish-identified interfaith family celebrates Christmas as a secular holiday only, heavy on the eggnog?

This is a tough call, and it can be made only on an individual basis. Whereas interfaith couples raising their children as Christians seem to have no problem putting a Hanukkah *menorah* on display alongside the Christmas stockings and mistletoe, Jewish-identified couples have to determine what ties they will retain to Christmas and other non-Jewish holidays and how the family's "minority viewpoint" parent will be accommodated. "Christmas trees come up at *every* meeting, even the ones we hold in July," notes Monica Andres, a Christian woman married to a Jewish man, who coordinates a discussion group for interfaith couples at a large Reform temple in Washington, D.C. "It's definitely a potent symbol, and causes a lot of discussion—or trouble—if one spouse is uncomfortable with it."

Elliott remembers vividly how his "one culture only" family grappled with the issue:

> My parents agreed that we would be raised Jewish. We celebrated the major Jewish holidays, and we celebrated Hanukkah with my father's family, and exchanged gifts among the kids. My parents didn't give us Hanukkah gifts, but my Jewish aunts and uncles did. On Christmas, we would get Christmas gifts from my parents, and we also visited my mother's family. We even had a tree. My [born-Jewish] father was an enthusiastic participant in the whole thing.
>
> By the time I was eight or nine years old, I had this sense of weirdness about having a tree, because other Jewish kids on the block didn't. They took Hanukkah more seriously than we did. So when the time came for the tree to go out to the garbage, I felt—especially as I grew older—uncomfortable with it being out there on the street, advertising the whole dilemma.

Elliott's Jewish father at least tried to acknowledge his converted wife's past. What happens in "only one" families in which the other culture is totally ignored? We've found that in interfaith marriages in which one spouse agrees to convert to the other's religion, or downplays or abandons all of his or her own religious practices, the children usually are acutely aware that Mom or Dad gave up something in order to remain in the marriage. While conversion may be willingly sought by the "minority" spouse, the children sometimes see it as unfair, and may perceive that parent as not really belonging to the ethnicity to which they've converted.

This was poignantly demonstrated at a forum for interfaith families at which the featured speaker was a prominent Reform rabbi—himself married to a Jew-by-choice—who is active in the outreach movement. When the rabbi contended that children of intermarriage who are being raised as Jews should have little contact with their Christian grandparents, and should not be permitted to visit them at Christmas or Easter, Robin objected. She noted that she herself had been raised as a "real" Christian, wholly cut off from Judaism, with a Jewish mother who had converted to Christianity, and that had not prevented her from living as a Jew once the truth about her background became known.

Discomfited, the rabbi sought to change the subject. With obvious relief, he gave the floor to a young boy, perhaps ten years old, who was sitting with his parents and three adorable, blond younger brothers. His *kipah* perched unsteadily on his head, the boy pointed at Robin and said indignantly, "That lady's right! Why can't my mommy have a Christmas tree? She's not a Jew! It isn't fair!" His horrified father issued a sharp rebuke to the boy. His mother looked down at the floor and then smiled tenderly at her son, tears filling her eyes. The boy's parents may have chosen to allow only one faith in their home, but his mother's mixed feelings about this had obviously reached him.

"No parent whose children are being raised in the religion

of the other parent should feel 'offended' or 'left out,' "
confidently assert the co-authors of a recent book for interfaith families. Perhaps these "out-parents" *shouldn't* feel that
way, but very often they *do,* as this young boy and a great
many adult descendants of intermarriage have indicated.
"My mother feels she has failed herself and me by my conversion to Judaism," says Nina. Raised as a Roman Catholic
in a religiously mixed community, Nina was allowed to associate with her Jewish relatives. Yet, despite Nina's decision
to affiliate as a Jew, her mother continues to pressure her to
attend Mass.

Nina's mother apparently thought that providing a Catholic home would guarantee her a permanently Catholic child.
She's not alone in this belief. Many materials dealing with
outreach to interfaith families insist that children raised
solely in one culture will become "real" Jews or "real" Christians as adults, without any external or internal conflicts,
and without the possibility of switching identities in
adulthood.

There is only one problem with this strategy. As the rest
of this book confirms, it doesn't really work the way its
architects intended. Of those we interviewed who were
raised solely as Jews or as Christians, the majority report
ongoing feelings of duality. As adults, some children of intermarriage say that regardless of how they were brought
up, they feel so drawn by their other "half" that they rather
dramatically jump ship to follow their feelings, switching
from Christianity to Judaism, perhaps, or from Judaism to
Unitarianism, or from a secular "nothing" life to something
that's more satisfying. . . .

Raise 'em in both cultures. This group advocates bringing
up the children with full exposure to both Jewish and Christian culture and traditions. Although 19 percent of those we
interviewed reported that they were "raised in both," most
said that their interfaith parents had not presented more

than a spotty, superficial view of Judaism and Christianity. "As I was raised as 'both,' I sometimes have felt that I had the best of both worlds, but nothing meaningful from either," remarked Susan, the daughter of a Jewish man and a woman who was herself the daughter of a Protestant-Catholic couple.

Many of today's advocates of a comprehensive Jewish/Christian upbringing are going much further than interfaith parents of previous generations. Recognizing the difficulty of shunting one parent's background into the background, these interfaith couples strive diligently to raise their children truly as "both."

"Within those interfaith families that have made such a commitment, there's an infectious spirit of pride and enthusiasm about their choice. Because there's no programmed religious life to hand their children, they've had to thoughtfully address and create it themselves, and in that effort, they've been able to grow in their understanding—and acceptance—of their spouse's roots as well as their own," stresses Lee F. Gruzen. An Episcopalian married to a Jew, Gruzen is raising her young daughters in both religious traditions, and has written a book to help other couples who wish to do the same (see page 205). Gruzen is at the forefront of a movement of interfaith parents who are tackling the duality issue head-on.

With such sensitivity and effort expended on them, the children of intermarriage are bound to have easier childhoods than preceding generations did. They may be over-endowed with religious and ethnic choices, but at least their families are aware of the duality struggles they're facing, and are doing their best to help resolve them. "The expectation is of workability, ninety percent of the time," says Gruzen. "When the conflicts come up—and they come up in a thousand ways—there are opportunities to keep bringing our fears to the surface, dealing with them, and growing with them. To see an interfaith marriage as a permanent separation that cannot be bridged, or as a pathology, is a sick and self-perpetuating attitude, in my opinion."

The jury is still out on how the children of intermarriage who are genuinely raised as "both" will affiliate and feel about their dual heritages when they reach adulthood. Since most of the current baby boomlet among interfaith couples hasn't yet reached the age of confirmation or *bar* or *bat mitzvah*, it will be twenty years or more until we have the benefit of hindsight. And in their strenuous efforts to play fair, many partners in "raise 'em in both" families do not or cannot think ahead to the day in which their children actually *do* make their choices. An abstract concept will become concrete, a number of interfaith couples have told us, when their children mature and decide upon Judaism or Christianity. Their open-mindedness notwithstanding, these parents divulge that they are surprised by how deeply hurt, even rejected, they feel by the early signs that their children may favor their spouse's heritage over their own.

In addition, unlike parents who share the same religious orientation, interfaith couples who truly desire to raise their children as "both" need to expend double the effort—and they may not have double the fun. Observing two sets of holidays, teaching the kids about two very different religious cultures, and visiting two houses of worship, even on an irregular basis, all add up to a lot of work, much of which may fall disproportionately on the mother's shoulders, just as it often does in "single-faith" homes.

Although the out-marriage rate among Jewish women is rising faster than it is for Jewish men, to date the majority of intermarriages involve Jewish men with Christian women. We've observed that these husbands frequently expect their born-Gentile wives to instill an age-appropriate Jewish awareness, if not a full Jewish identity, in their little children, a task for which these mothers may be ill-prepared.

At times, this husbandly expectation appears to stretch motherly intuition beyond its natural limits. "When Ed heard me tell our four-year-old that Hanukkah was the name of a brave Jewish general, he just about hit the roof. But I notice *he's* not doing much to give the kids a Jewish education," mutters Trish, a Roman Catholic who's raising her children with exposure to both traditions. "In some respects, he knows as little about Jewish customs as I do, but somehow I'm just expected to know."

Raise 'em in a third culture, or in no culture. Family tensions cannot be sidestepped even in interfaith families in which no religious culture is maintained beyond cursory nods toward Christmas, Easter, Hanukkah, and Passover, or in which a third belief system, such as Ethical Culture or Buddhism, has been adopted. According to the 23 percent of our respondents who were raised as "nothing" or in a third, "compromise" culture, their parents' refusal to teach them much about their pasts—usually on the grounds that religious and ethnic roots are "no big deal"—served merely to bewilder them and to infuriate or sadden both of their extended families.

Lacking roots as children, we may have trouble coaxing them to grow as adults. Sally says that she was told by her Jewish mother and Baptist father that she was a Jew, yet she was raised as "nothing." Now in her midforties, she and one other sibling identify as Jews, one is Unitarian, and another is a Christian of unspecified denomination. "I do not care for religion," says Sally. "I feel it breeds prejudice. I do believe in the Jewish heritage, but religion has no meaning for me."

Compared with the secularly reared adult children of same-faith homes, the descendants of secular interfaith homes appear to have a more difficult time as adults in defining and asserting their identities. Simone's parents did not observe any home-based religious rituals but allowed

her plenty of access to her Jewish mother's relatives. Despite
this, she says:

> As a child, I felt confused and left out when I was with
> my Jewish cousins, who all went to temple and studied
> Hebrew. During the High Holidays when I sat in temple
> all day long, I did not know what was going on. I wanted
> to know more, but felt ashamed *not* to know.
>
> With my Christian cousins, I was equally left out, be-
> cause they went to church. Although I celebrated Christ-
> mas and Easter, it was void of any religious meaning. As
> I got older, I actively sought out information about religions
> in general and attended many different churches.

Simone married a Catholic man from Eastern Europe and
converted to his faith. "Though we are raising our children
as Catholics, they're also being taught about their Jewish
heritage, so they can be proud of what they are," she says.

Trina would applaud Simone's wise decision. Raised as
"nothing," she says:

> I feel strongly that the children born of an intermarriage
> should be exposed to both parents' religions. Children are
> very accepting and open-hearted and will not be confused
> in the long run—at least, not any more than adults are!
>
> However, if you don't learn religious practices in child-
> hood, you'll never feel comfortable with them if you want
> to pick them up as an adult. My [secular Jewish] father
> was never taught to be a Jew, so he could not pass being
> Jewish on to me. I cannot pass it on to my daughter, and
> so I feel a double loss.

Raising children in a third culture that is new to both
parents may create additional tension in a family that's trying
to sidestep the identity issue altogether. Interfaith couples

often try to find a safe, noncontroversial harbor in Unitarianism, Quakerism, or some other muted version of Christianity. This path has become so common that it's almost palatable to some Jewish families whose children have "married out." While Unitarianism is not Judaism, the grandparents rationalize, at least their grandchildren will be raised in a low-key, inoffensive environment that is not showily "Christian" and that preaches racial and religious tolerance.

However, if neither parent is deeply rooted in the new "compromise" culture, it may appear shallow and meaningless to their children, who may express intense curiosity about what they perceive as their *real* backgrounds, our respondents have disclosed. "My parents raised me as a Unitarian," says Ned, son of a Jewish man and a Methodist woman. "They kept talking about what a good compromise it was. That made me kind of contemptuous, because I didn't want to be a compromise myself." When he was in his late twenties, Ned chose to undergo a Conservative Jewish conversion.

In some cases, attempting to circumvent the conflicting requirements of Judaism and Christianity yields near-comic results. A Jewish woman from New York City, married to a German Catholic man, once told us that they had opted to join the pagan movement, a modern revival of European "white magic" matriarchal witchcraft. The woman noted proudly that the child they hoped to have would be raised as a *"real* pagan," insisting that paganism would give the child a single identity, freeing him or her from the influence of the Jewish family she abhorred.

Like many other interfaith parents, this pagan-come-lately had yet to discover that none of these strategies—raise 'em in just one religion; raise 'em in both; choose a third culture, or raise 'em as "nothing"—works as well as their advocates would like. We would venture to say that it is probably impossible to produce an adult child of intermarriage who feels that he or she fits snugly in one culture, exhibiting *no* curiosity whatsoever about their "other half."

Raising a child in both cultures, and expecting that as an adult this individual will just know unambiguously where he or she belongs, shows greater awareness of our duality, but fails to recognize that our ultimate choice is based on some extremely complex cues. Introducing a child to a third culture complicates rather than simplifies the situation. And choosing to bring up a child of intermarriage as "nothing" forces him or her to start from scratch in forming an identity. As an adult, he or she can spend years playing catch-up in an unfamiliar culture, or may reject the whole process as hopelessly arduous or personally meaningless.

"So tell us," exasperated interfaith couples often ask, "what is the best way to raise our children? What *is* the 'magic bullet'?" The answer is that interfaith parents must become aware that for their children, duality is a given, and that it has a life of its own, negotiated through a series of *normal* developmental stages that cannot be avoided. Some of us may be hardly aware that we are passing through these stages, but indeed we are.

Moreover, even when our final choices are made, we never fully blot out one parental culture. We simply have a primary identity and a secondary identity (or more!), which coexist within a single personality. We are like a pair of stereo speakers, one of which may transmit more sound than the other. Let's look at this process through our respondents' childhood memories.

How the children see it. Whatever decisions our interfaith parents make regarding our birth ceremonies and how we will be raised, their feelings, and those of our relatives, become more obvious to us as we mature. As young children, we may not be able to articulate precisely what we are seeing, but we are nonetheless acutely aware of our families' feelings. Our parents and relatives personify our two worlds.

"Amazingly enough, the sense that our family was different was a palpable presence with me from about the age of six," says Joyce, who grew up in a small southern town in which her father's Jewish background was not known. "I can remember thinking that perhaps my father was black, in spite of conclusive evidence to the contrary. It was a very confusing environment for me as a child—to know what I didn't really know, and to sense what I wasn't supposed to be aware of."

Despite the best intentions of our interfaith parents, no matter how they raise us, we often find that our relatives and society in general offer no room for concession. Plainspoken grandparents and other relatives leave us in no doubt as to their feelings. If their culture predominates in our homes, we often see them spar with the parent whose background is minimized ("Who gave Rachel that Easter basket?"). If their beliefs are excluded from our lives, we are made aware of their sorrow and resentment. Jim's Jewish grandfather covertly took steps to change this situation to his satisfaction. Jim, one of nine children born to a German Catholic man and an emotionally fragile Jewish woman, recalls:

> My folks had agreed to raise us as Catholics, but my Jewish grandfather didn't agree. Whenever my mother was ill, I was sent over to my grandfather's place, and he would secretly teach me about Judaism. He said that my Catholic education wasn't right, that I was a Jew and should know about Judaism.

Because of the mixed messages we receive from our extended families and from society in general, many children of intermarriage develop a nagging, persistent sense of being not "as good" as other people—their all-Jewish or all-Christian cousins, for example. Such feelings are a direct

40

result of society's inability to recognize how someone can have more than one primary ethnic or religious allegiance. Duality is viewed as odd or bad. These beliefs are aggravated by the curiosity of friends, and by those people and institutions that regard our duality as a disorder. (One Hebrew-school registration form we've seen sandwiches interfaith family status between check-off boxes for allergies and dyslexia.)

Christian parochial schools may send disturbingly anti-Semitic messages of their own, even if communicated in a joking manner. Margaret Mary, a Catholic woman in her forties, remembers this scene from her childhood:

> We were studying for a state exam. The nun said, "Now, let's be sure and study hard so we beat those smart Jewish kids." I didn't know what to do. I felt creepy. You see, my mother is Jewish, and the nun didn't know that.

Ursula, another Catholic-reared child of intermarriage, remembers that her "half-breed status" created problems among her classmates at a convent school. Noting that she was "not well trusted" because of her mixed background, "they called me 'little dirty Jew girl' and made me do the chores." Ursula remained loyal to Catholicism until "age seventeen, when I changed, because I found no peace there. I felt that I had no real place, because there were problems in both [the Jewish and the Christian] communities. I now consider myself a Hebrew Christian."

Reconciling her parents' cultures also resulted in peer pressure for Sara, the daughter of a Greek Orthodox man and a Jewish woman who had converted to Greek Orthodoxy. Raised solely as a Christian, Sara learned of her status as a child of intermarriage "when I was about six, I guess. I found out my mother wasn't actually Greek. My Jewish cousins taunted me about a statue of the Virgin Mary in my room.

My school friends, who were Catholic, wouldn't speak to me when they found out I was Jewish."

In sum, regardless of how our family chooses to deal—or not to deal—with the presence of two parental cultures, many of us have been aware of our "differentness" since we were toddlers. Our recollections can remain vivid for many decades, as Milton attests. Now in his sixties, he recalls, "When I was two or three, my [Jewish] father's mother spat on my head and called me a *shaygetz*. Then my parents explained the term"—a pejorative word for a non-Jew.

There *is* much to explain in an interfaith family, and much to do. To nurture psychologically healthy children and grandchildren of Jewish-Gentile intermarriage, there are no quick-fix ways to integrate our two "halves," and ignoring them is no solution either. But do accompany us on our travels. If the endogamously raised world learns to confront, accept, and understand what may be a frighteningly alien concept—the abiding, *perfectly normal* presence of our duality, no matter how we are raised—the children of intermarriage have a far better chance of achieving a harmoniously balanced adult identity.

CHAPTER

3

Second Thoughts, Second Choices, as We Come to Maturity

As a child I thought I would be Christian like my mother. As a teenager, I thought of converting to Judaism when I realized I didn't believe in Christ as God. However, when I investigated and found the Jewish religion to be sexist, I changed to being an agnostic.

—SASHA, SYSTEMS ANALYST

I vacillated constantly between Judaism and Episcopalianism during adolescence, a crisis that resulted in several years of soul-searching. I was reluctant to make a formal conversion to Christianity, but when I was in college, I finally did. I think what I longed for most of all was a way to embrace both "halves" without having to sacrifice either one.

—MARGIE, EDITOR

WHEN I ARRIVED AT THE UNIVERSITY OF CALIFORNIA AT Berkeley for my freshman year, I was primed to begin a new life—a Jewish life! Summoning all my courage, I introduced myself to a rabbi enjoying the fall sunshine at a Chabad House card table in Sproul Plaza, the site of the Free Speech Movement's greatest battles during the 1960s. I told him that I'd received no Jewish education, except that which I'd been able to pick up on my own, and that I was looking to learn more and to live Jewishly.

"That's wonderful, Leslie," said the rabbi, obviously pleased by my enthusiasm. But when I explained that my father was Jewish and my mother was Gentile—I hadn't

43

thought it might behoove me to conceal this fact—he frowned at me, as though I'd set out to deceive him. "There is no place in Judaism for you," the rabbi said curtly, and turned back to the book he'd been reading.

Although I felt deeply hurt and chastened at the time, now I laugh when I recall that goofy girl, too naïve to suspect that a Lubavitcher Hasid would be extremely unlikely to welcome the unconverted daughter of a Gentile mother into the Jewish community, even on probationary terms. The experience taught me to say as little as possible to "born" Jews about my background, and thereafter I passed as a secular Jew intent on catching up on her religious education. At best, concealing my dual nature so strenuously was unpleasant; at worst, I felt as though I were masquerading as something I could never truly be.

In my youthful ignorance, I assumed that few others had to choose a primary religious and cultural identity. But in later years, and while researching this book, Robin and I found that many other teenage and young-adult children of intermarriage experience the same sort of confusion, rejection, and discomfort as they attempt to decide where they belong. As we decode the admission requirements for a Jewish or Christian milieu that may be attractive to us, we may find its practices dauntingly unfamiliar.

With its emphasis on proselytizing, Christianity accommodates newcomers fairly easily, although as teenagers or young adults we still need to summon up courage in order to approach a Christian youth group or church on our own, without our families behind us. Judaism appears particularly impenetrable, our interviewees say, with its Hebrew prayers and Yiddish slang, its emphasis on family-centered, home-based rituals, and its suspicion of outsiders.

My unsettling encounter with the Hasid took place nearly twenty years ago. A great many Jews and Christians have told us that the confusion and rejection many adult children

44

of intermarriage report facing simply wouldn't occur in today's climate, which they presume is more tolerant of religious and ethnic diversity.

Christianity, these observers point out, is much more accepting of the children of intermarriage than in earlier eras. And most Jews assume that even under the strictest definition of Jewish law, the offspring of Jewish mothers and Gentile fathers are universally accepted by other Jews, magically free of identity conflicts. As for the teenage children of Jewish fathers and Gentile mothers, who are not considered Jewish under *halacha*, Jews ask us, aren't their concerns adequately dealt with nowadays by the outreach programs for interfaith couples and converts that were created by Reform and Reconstructionist Judaism in the late 1970s?

If she were to speak with these well-meaning Christians and Jews, Emily would surely challenge their complacency. A slender, fair-haired widow in her late forties, of northern European descent, she once sought us out, after we'd spoken at a Reform Jewish temple, to ask what we thought about her two teenagers' situation.

Emily explained that after she and her Orthodox Jewish–reared husband had married, she had fulfilled her promise to him to raise their children solely as Reform Jews, permitting them little contact with her Protestant relatives. Eventually, she and her husband stopped buying Christmas trees for their home. Emily never attended church, worshipping only at Reform Jewish services with her husband, and converted to Judaism soon after her husband died, when her children entered their teens.

But now there was trouble. Enthusiastic about his Jewish heritage, her son had opted to attend a university that had a large Jewish enrollment. He told Emily that when his two dormitory roommates—both from strongly traditional Jewish homes—learned that his mother had been born a Gentile, they'd announced, "We'd never let our daughters marry someone like you." Although deeply hurt, Emily's son remained resolved to live as a Jew.

When her daughter learned of this incident, said Emily, "she became very quiet. Then she asked me if I would send her to visit my relatives in Europe. She had never met them, because travel is so expensive, but we had kept in touch by mail." When her daughter returned from her summer abroad, she told her mother, "Your family is wonderful. I even look like them. I feel at home in their culture. *They're my people!*"

Emily looked at us imploringly. "It's true, she *does* resemble my family. She won't go to synagogue at all now. Should I make her go?" No, we ventured. Don't force her. "What about your son?" Robin asked. "Well, he's like his father," she replied. "Dark. Determined. He wants to visit Israel. He's studying hard and plans to enter the rabbinate. He clings to Judaism."

During adolescence, our growing autonomy from our parents gives us the freedom to explore our "two halves," to dabble in Judaism and Christianity, or to take hesitant steps upon other spiritual paths. We listen closely, in order to hear which way of life calls to us most loudly. Even if our parents' life patterns are determinedly secular, we constantly receive two sets (and sometimes more) of ethnic, cultural messages. We have breathed them in all our lives, they are part of our daily bread, served alongside Aunt Kirsten's *lutefisk* and Bubbe's *matzah brei*.

It doesn't matter whether the teenager in question is a secular child of a Jewish father, knocking at the Jewish community's door, or the child of a Jewish mother who feels strongly drawn by Catholicism, or an atheist with one Jewish parent who nevertheless would like to feel ethnically secure *somewhere*. Adolescence is the time when we begin to decide what we want to be, spiritually and ethnically, when we grow up. Recipients of yet another conflict, in addition to all the others that mark these turbulent years, the children of intermarriage embark on a unique identity search, a journey that their interfaith parents can observe and influence, but in which they cannot actively participate.

Our parents' problems with us. If they come from single-faith homes, our parents are ill-equipped to help us, as they lack firsthand experience in dealing with dual identities. As former adolescents themselves, interfaith parents can draw on their memories as well as on their own good judgment in walking the tightrope between permissiveness and undue strictness on such typical teen issues as hair styles, table manners, and curfews. But regulating *belief* and *identity*—if, indeed, such things can be "regulated"—is much harder.

As their children mature, interfaith couples are forced to confront their own attitudes about religion and ethnicity. For many, it may be the first time such issues have been explored in depth since the couple confronted—or evaded—the issue at the time of their wedding or upon the births of their children. For those like Emily and her husband, who chose to feature only one religious culture in the home, adolescence may be the time when parents witness their offspring's rejection in one ethnic community, or when the children consider switching over to the culture that was erased from the home. This can be extremely painful for conscientious Jews-by-choice like Emily, for Jews who have converted to Christianity, or for interfaith couples who have chosen to lead secular lives. All must watch helplessly as their teenage offspring enthusiastically embrace the culture they themselves abandoned.

"My parents each had rebelled against organized religion," says Charlotte, whose born-Jewish mother became an agnostic as an adult, as did her Lutheran-reared father. "So how was I to rebel? By having a religious crisis when I was

47

thirteen." Charlotte began attending an Episcopalian church "because it was the closest. And I liked the hymns and the services." However, she adds:

> I couldn't swallow the theology. I began to get indigestion and feelings of malaise on weekends. The family doctor diagnosed it as "menstrual," and prescribed sedatives. (He thought everything was menstrual.) One day my mother, quite out of the blue, said to me, "You don't have to go to church," and I realized I was never going to have that sickness again, and I stopped going to church. It was one of the most insightful things that she ever did or said to me.
>
> Some months later, she did some legwork and discovered that there was an active Ethical Culture group in town, so I went. It was fun. I made some good friends in the Sunday school. There was an odd thing about it, though— I was never clear on what Ethical Culture really was. Our topic at that time was comparative religion.
>
> At the age of fifteen, I began to attend the Unitarian youth group. I liked that better because there were more older boys. I remember studying the New Testament from a scientific, not devotional, point of view, and I liked that.

Like Charlotte's parents, interfaith couples often see their teenagers act independently to contact institutions, grandparents, and other relatives for information and support in affiliating with a culture other than the one that was selected for them. Teens also might opt to go with the flow, like Martha, the daughter of a Jewish mother and born-Gentile father, who notes, "I remember wanting to be a WASP as a preteen. I think I wanted to fit in with my peers. This stage passed, however," and Martha became a *bat mitzvah* in Jerusalem.

For those couples who have bought time by saying, "We'll

let the children choose what they want to be when they grow up," the long-deferred bill may be coming due. Interfaith parents who have explored both cultures extensively within their family may watch with dismay as their children express an active preference for a particular religious or ethnic identity, leaving one parent out in the cold. If religious ritual holds no intrinsic value for an interfaith couple, it can be an equally wrenching experience when their adolescent expresses interest in *any* religious affiliation ceremony, such as confirmation, baptism, or *bar* or *bat mitzvah*. Even teenagers' entry into nonreligiously oriented Jewish or Christian groups can be unexpectedly jarring for secular parents who have no interest in their birth cultures.

It is not uncommon for *both* parents to experience the "loss" of an adolescent child who explores a third spiritual path, such as Buddhism. As teens, the children of intermarriage may consider selecting a faith that is altogether different from either parent's. The confusion felt by many of these teenagers, irrespective of their ultimate choices, is clearly described by Marie, the daughter of a Jewish man and Presbyterian woman, who said:

> I was sent to a Presbyterian Sunday school from ages six to thirteen, so I would have some exposure to religion. I left that church when confirmation prep began. . . . I wanted to maintain contact with both traditions, as an expression of a need to be close and loyal to both families. Even as my decision to identify myself as a Christian developed, I didn't think of myself as a non-Jew—I am both a Jew and a Christian in terms of family values.

Our problems with our parents. Teenagers often find that even innocent questions about their interfaith family's background can be met by vague, dismissive, or testy responses. And no matter how they have been raised, adolescents, who are already hypersensitive to what they perceive as the hypocrisy of the adult world, may use religious and ethnic identity issues ("Well, what *am* I, anyway?") as a means of aggravating their elders.

Conversely, teenagers who already walk gingerly around their interfaith parents may avoid the issues of religion and ethnicity altogether during their last years at home, for fear of upsetting them further. Since children of intermarriage are already placed in the position of "rejecting" a parent when they opt to identify as a Jew or a Christian, many teens postpone this decision, in order to maintain at least one peaceful point of contact during a stormy period of life. (This reluctance to identify may remain a constant in one's adult life. As we'll discuss in subsequent chapters, a substantial number of the adult children of intermarriage we queried said that it has been impossible to find an agreeable niche in religious or secular groups in either the Jewish *or* the Christian community.)

Divide and conquer. Issues that endogamous couples can tackle as a united front may divide interfaith parents, who, unfortunately, cannot as easily hide behind blanket statements. Take, for example, interfaith dating. In a 1981 survey of two hundred teenage girls, conducted by *Seventeen* magazine, an astounding 97 percent said that religion played no part in determining whom they dated. Two Jewish parents or two Catholic parents who disapprove of interdating may be able to express their feelings as a unit. But the teenager's favorite H-word—hypocrisy—may be prompted if an interfaith couple, raising their children as "real" Jews or "real" Christians, shows strong disapproval of interdating. Their offspring are likely, as teenagers, to seek information about the family's suppressed, minority viewpoint by befriending and dating members of that culture.

A partner in an interfaith marriage—especially one who takes pride in not being particularly religious—may receive a nasty jolt when his or her child rejects the stereotypical characteristics of that parent's background. The marked contrast between herself and her tall, blond, WASPy-looking teenage daughter stung Sonny Wainwright, a dark-haired, dark-eyed, Jewish lesbian feminist poet and writer who was briefly married to a Christian man. Wainwright wrote:

> I fashioned this gift for her. There is
>> love for studying, books, and reverence
>>> of Jewish ancestry . . .
>
>> Revered books and love for studying
>> are rejected for horseback riding.
>> Her life is not given to love for learning.
>> She hates school and leaves me diminished . . .
>
>> My values are rejected for horseback riding:
>> my child is not me . . .
>> I wish she were not Episcopalian
>> on her father's side.

The conflicting messages transmitted by our interfaith parents may seem trivial or even comical. But they greatly increase the normal adolescent burden of guilt and confusion, which is reflected in similar emotions on the part of the parents that they may not be able to express verbally. Sometimes an interfaith parent unconsciously sabotages the family's efforts to establish a "house religion" by denigrating the other parent's culture, or by letting the teenager know that it's all right to abandon it. This behavior may take such forms as abruptly reneging on an agreement to raise a child as a Jew or as a Christian, or by refusing to allow the child to have a long-planned confirmation or *bar* or *bat mitzvah*. The sabotaging parent is telling the teenager that at least one child is going to belong to that parent's culture, not to the other parent's world.

"My folks may have, at a certain point, asked me if I wanted a *bar mitzvah*," remarks Elliott, who recalls his surprise at learning that his parents did not plan to prepare him for the ceremony. He discovered as an adult that his mother had refused to allow it, despite her promise to keep a Jewish home. He noted:

> I only began to discuss the subject with my mother a few months ago. I was really surprised, because she expressed feelings of guilt about contributing to a situation that has led to confusion for me. She said that she and my father had agreed that I would not be *bar mitzvah*. That came as big news to me, because I had no idea that that had been the case. I still want to explore that more with her, but even today, my curiosity is threatening to her.

Elliott defines his family as relatively normal and happy, but this harmony did not exempt him and his sister from a sabotage attempt. (Reconciling his two halves "remains a problem for me," says Elliott, who has been in therapy for many years.)

Looking at our parents. If our parents are taking a new look at each other and at us, we, in turn, are subjecting them to our first real adult scrutiny. Our interfaith parents often expect that we'll be little multicultural ambassadors of goodwill, with "rainbows in our souls." Instead, they find that their teenager is capable of delivering a devastatingly critical assessment of *both* their worlds at the breakfast table.

Daniel, a college student, sees his two worlds quite unsentimentally. Raised by a Jewish father and a formerly Protestant mother who converted to Judaism, he says:

> For the first couple of years of Hebrew school, I was determined to grow up to be a practicing Jew, but I lost interest in that before my *bar mitzvah*, after which it didn't

concern me much. I think the whole appeal of being religious to me at such an early age was the approval it brought from my father and religious schoolteachers. My mother was totally supportive of my desire to be religious when I was young. That's just the way she is.

As Daniel matured, he found himself gravitating more toward his mother's family.

I definitely do feel sometimes like there are two halves existing between me, or at least that I was raised in two separate worlds. Because my parents divorced when I was young, I grew up in the two environments separately. . . . I try my best to be like my mother's family for a number of reasons. I don't want to come off as some self-hating Alex Portnoy Jew, but I guess my background gives me the right to be honest.

I am convinced that my mother's family has more class than my father's family. Whether this is universally true of the two religions, or just true for the differences between my mother and father, doesn't really matter to me. I have already said how my mother's family would be supportive of almost anything I did, and this is just one reason why I try to emulate them.

My [Protestant] maternal grandparents' house is always filled with happy, intellectual conversation. They are exceptionally polite. They don't talk about money. They also have the most profound respect for privacy. . . . My [Jewish] father's family is different. They talk openly about money, in a manner I consider kind of tacky. . . . My Jewish family is also grossly overprotective.

So anyway, I try to act like my non-Jewish family more than my Jewish family. . . . I would like to marry a non-Jewish girl and raise the children according to her religion. I would tell them I was a Unitarian, and go play golf on Sunday mornings.

While Daniel's views have been sharpened by his parents' divorce, as well as by the conspicuous dissimilarity of the two families, his ability to coolly assess the differences between his two worlds is typical of the teenage children of intermarriage.

The best of both? Our interfaith parents anticipate that we will receive the best of both worlds—perhaps because they can't bear to think otherwise—and some of us are indeed proud of our dual status. For example, one interfaith couple bemusedly told us about their teenage son, raised as a "real" Jew, whose favorite sweatshirt, which he wears even to Jewish youth activities, is emblazoned with the logo of the University of Notre Dame, an affecting tribute to his Catholic-reared mother. ("He wants to identify with a winning team," a friend of the couple pointed out.)

Yet, even when they've come to maturity, presumably more willing to cut the old folks some slack, some descendants of intermarriage still rankle when they recall their interfaith parents' flip efforts to rationalize their situation. "My [Jewish] father used to say to us, 'Don't worry, hybrids are stronger,' " notes Joyce, who was raised as a Presbyterian. His remark "was neither a consolation nor inspiration to me. I always felt like a stalk of disease-resistant corn. My sister and I always referred to ourselves as 'half-breeds.' "

That's a label of sorts, though hardly a satisfying one. And how teenagers love labels! The right sweater or the coolest shoes can mean everything to someone who yearns for approval. So it can be doubly difficult for children of interfaith parents to proclaim, in a form that their peers will understand and accept, just what they are. Not surprisingly, teenage Holly, among others, gets a trifle pugnacious about her status as a child of intermarriage. "If someone knows, they know," she says. "If they don't like it, well, that's tough."

Even in a secular environment, in which religion per se is not emphasized, teenagers are unsure how they'll be received. The stresses multiplied for Louise, the daughter of a Jewish woman and Catholic man, who exclaims:

> I was raised in complete confusion! I knew I was both Jewish and Gentile. Until the age of eleven, we lived in a Gentile neighborhood, and I was teased and called names for being a Jew. Then we moved to a Jewish neighborhood where the Gentile side of me was never accepted.
>
> In high school, I was pledged to what was considered the most inferior Jewish sorority, because I was only half-Jewish and my [maiden] name was Clark. Even though I was a good student, very active in sports, and a cheerleader, I was never accepted as a whole person.

Older adolescents also can have trouble grasping the "two halves" of a descendant of intermarriage. That was certainly the case for Joanne, who recalls sourly that during her stint at a Big Ten university, a prestigious Gentile sorority blackballed her because her father was Jewish, while a Jewish house balked at pledging a member whose mother was Christian. Coming at such a vulnerable, receptive time in our lives, such rejection may have far-reaching effects on our self-image. Now in her fifties, Joanne says she still has a hard time feeling comfortable in Jewish *or* Christian circles.

Experiencing the worst that both of our worlds has to offer is likely to leave us feeling puzzled, yet fiercely protective of our interfaith parents. Julie says:

> I am an atheist, although among family and friends I call myself a "halfsie." I always assumed that I would remain a Lutheran, as I was raised, but the turning point came when the minister told me in confirmation class, in front of twenty other thirteen-year-olds, that my father would burn in hell because he was Jewish and had never been baptized. But I *knew* my father was a good person.

Try as we might, as adolescents we cannot shield our interfaith parents from all the unpleasantness to which our family status may subject us. They, in turn, cannot fully protect us from the outside world—or from any trouble at home.

For some of us, our teen years are when we first become painfully aware that something that we once perceived as merely a quirk may actually indicate major family problems. As we'll explore in chapters 7 and 8, teens from stressed or dysfunctional interfaith homes may find that their bicultural parents respond *very* differently to crises, while our two extended families are likely to blame any discord on the intermarriage rather than on the problem itself. And as we venture beyond our parents' doorsteps, we are likely to encounter hurdles that complicate our entry into either or both of our two worlds.

Half-Jews, half-Christians? If we seek to explore the Christian world for the first time as teenagers or young adults, we may have to explain why others in our interfaith family have not accepted Jesus. Worse still, we may experience anti-Semitism, whether subtle or blatant.

For young descendants of intermarriage who are interested in learning more about their Jewish "half," our status problems are likely to be exacerbated by the ongoing battle over the question, "Who is a Jew?" This question has plagued patrilineal descendants of intermarriage of all ages (and even some matrilineals, too) who consider identifying as Jews. Briefly, to those who are trying to decide, "Am I—or should I be—Jewish, Christian, or something else?", the Jewish community currently offers *five* conflicting answers:

• **Israel's Law of Return** provides automatic Israeli citizenship to any immigrating Jew, defined as a person with a biological Jewish mother, or a person who has converted to Judaism. Right-wing Israeli groups are currently lobbying to tighten the language of this law in order to disallow Reform and Conservative conversions, and to stamp the passports of such converts with the word *ger,* Hebrew for "convert."

• **Orthodox Jews** forbid intermarriage between a Jew and an unconverted Gentile. Only the biological children of a born-Jewish mother or the children of a Gentile woman converted to Judaism through Orthodox ritual before their births are considered automatically Jewish. A child of a Gentile woman and a Jewish man must be converted according to *halacha,* which involves immersion in the *mikveh* as well as circumcision for males; the same goes for a Gentile child adopted by a Jewish couple. Some American Orthodox rabbis will not grant halachic conversions to the children of non-Orthodox parents, unless they promise to change their lives and maintain a traditional Jewish home—observing the Sabbath, keeping kosher, and so forth.

• **Conservative Judaism** strongly disapproves of intermarriage. The biological children of any Jewish woman are considered legitimate Jews, but the children of a Gentile woman must be converted unless she underwent the procedure—preferably under Orthodox or Conservative auspices—before her children were born. Unlike Orthodox rabbis, Conservative rabbis will consider some Reform or Reconstructionist conversions to be valid, depending on the circumstances. "No rabbinical body has a totally uniform position. In each case, the conversion procedure has to be looked at on its own merits, and then the rabbi will make a judgment call," says Rabbi Joel Meyers, executive director of the Rabbinical Assembly. Some Conservative rabbis say that they'll accept a Reform or Reconstructionist convert as long as he or she was immersed in the *mikveh,* for example, while others will not.

In any case, Conservative rabbis are unlikely to randomly conduct a background check on a family that leads a Jewish life. The issue of validity as a Conservative Jew arises, and conversion may be required, before a patrilineal child of intermarriage undergoes *bris* or baby naming, *bar* or *bat mitz-vah*, becomes a member of a Conservative synagogue, or is married by a Conservative rabbi.

• **The Reconstructionist movement,** a liberal offshoot of Conservative Judaism, voted in 1968 to accept the children of Jewish fathers and Gentile mothers as Jews; **Reform Judaism** followed suit in 1983. While neither of these denominations is pleased with the steep rise in Jewish-Gentile intermarriage, they are attempting to keep at least some interfaith families within Judaism by adopting this so-called patrilineal rule. In both denominations, the children must be raised as Jews from birth in order to be accepted as Jews. These liberal wings of Judaism accept Orthodox and Conservative conversions, as well as their own. However, Reform and Reconstructionist Judaism apparently offer no institutional "grandfather clause" admitting teenage and adult children of intermarriage who received secular or Christian upbringings, yet now consider themselves Jewish and wish to affiliate with a liberal temple and participate in its activities.

Here again, rabbis enjoy wide latitude as to whether they will consider such an individual a Jew or a non-Jew. Depending on the upbringing and level of education of a particular child of intermarriage, a rabbi might say, "Fine, come on in." Or, as in the experience of a number of our respondents—*including* a few matrilineals—who were raised as Christians or as "nothing," Reform or Reconstructionist rabbis might insist upon conversion before full status in the congregation will be granted.

• **The secular humanist wing of Judaism** accepts all persons of Jewish descent who define themselves as Jews, no questions asked.

Jewish definitions contradict, in turn, Islamic and Christian laws. The Islamic law of *Shari'ah* maintains that all children of Moslem fathers are Moslems (regardless of their mother's status), while Christians consider any descendant of Jewish-Christian intermarriage to be a Christian if that person has been baptized.

Teenagers and young adults may not absorb all these complexities at once, but it becomes clear to them very quickly that the divisions in their families over their identities reflect the outside world's discord. However a teenage child of intermarriage considers affiliating, feelings of dislocation are very likely to persist. Continuing the process that begins in childhood, teenage offspring of Jewish-Gentile intermarriage inevitably will continue to discover, in increasingly sophisticated ways, just how unpredictable, hypocritical, and unfair the world can be in general—and in religious and ethnic communities in particular. (We simply get more polite, or accepting, or withdrawn, about all this as we mature.)

For young adults, and for the parents and relatives who love them, we offer the following advice, distilled from the collective experience of hundreds of survivors of adolescence in interfaith families:

• **It is all right—even desirable, at times—to feel as though you have "two halves."** If you are a young adult coming of age in an interfaith home, bear in mind that it is *normal* to experience conflict over a dual identity. It is *not possible* to resolve all of your identity concerns as a teenager. You've already got enough to do. And teenage children of interfaith parents have very few role models in popular culture or in literature, and not many opportunities to discuss their unique status problems with others like themselves. As you mature, you'll have more power and opportunity to mold your life to your liking, however you choose to affiliate.

• **Bear in mind that your intermarried parents may be hypersensitive to your questions about your background.** If you're being raised primarily in one culture, and it satisfies you, by all means stay there, learn, and grow with it. But if you need more information about your "other half," ask your parents. Try not to turn a few simple questions into a heated confrontation. If your curiosity upsets your parents, don't browbeat them. Seek out a friendly relative for enlightenment. Wanting to know more about your Roman Catholic, Italian-American mother's family, for example, will not make you less legitimate as a Jew, if that is how you and your parents identify. Such knowledge *will* put you at ease with your background, and might give you insight into your personality, or allow you a preview of the kind of person you may become.

• **If your interfaith parents have expended a great deal of effort to raise you as a "real" Jew, a "real" Christian, a secular "citizen of the world," or any other affiliation, try to understand their emotional commitment to your future.** Interfaith parents have been known to put their children on display in order to demonstrate the "correctness" of their upbringing. Any instances in which you're asked to play Charlie McCarthy to your interfaith parents' Edgar Bergen are, ironically, a reflection of their natural love for and pride in you, and their earnest efforts to give you the right start in life. However, it puts an unfair pressure on you to deny any equally natural interest that you might have in either parent's heritage.

• **Don't be maneuvered into denigrating either of your "two halves."** You can be a good Jew, for example, and still have a sympathetic understanding of your Christian parent's background and beliefs. Conversely, if you enjoy the fellowship of your family's fundamentalist Christian church, you need not endorse missionary efforts to convert all the Jews.

• **Interfaith parents should remain calm while their teenage children try on different identities for size.** Many descendants of intermarriage have reported that as adults they've changed their minds more than once about their religious identity. Experimenting with new personalities and ways of life is a natural part of adolescence and young adulthood, however aggravating parents may find it. If you can't decide from week to week what you are, it doesn't mean that your interfaith parents didn't raise you properly—simply that your built-in religious, cultural, and ethnic duality is in full working order.

• **Become aware of the roots of possible parental "sabotage," but again, try to exercise some tact.** If you are interested in *bar* or *bat mitzvah* or confirmation, and yours has been canceled or put off with unconvincing excuses, discuss it with your parents. Try to find out why either or both fear your making a religious commitment. One reason is offered by Walter, the son of a Unitarian woman and a Jewish-turned-Unitarian man. Married to a Jewish woman, he says, "My daughter was raised Jewish, but she had no *bat mitzvah.* I objected because I felt it would separate her from me." If your parents balk at the notion of providing you with a coming-of-age ceremony, perhaps they need to be reassured that you'll always cherish them *and* their birth cultures, even if only one culture has your primary allegiance.

• **Interfaith parents for whom religion is "no big deal" frequently assume that their children feel the same way. If you don't, your parents won't know unless you tell them so.** If determining a primary identity is very important to you, but seemingly not to your parents, don't try to convert them, or to guilt-trip them into being more observant of the religious or ethnic traditions that matter most to you. It is *very* common for the children of secular, "no big deal" interfaith couples to feel much more strongly about religion and ethnicity than their parents do.

• **Find a sponsor.** If you wish to practice certain religious rituals that are unfamiliar or personally unacceptable to your parents, or if you're interested in participating in secular Jewish or Christian organizations, try to find someone to act as your guide. A friend, relative, or sympathetic clergyperson probably would be most effective in this capacity on neutral turf, away from the emotionally charged atmosphere of your interfaith family's home. If such a learning experience is difficult or impossible to arrange, remember that you'll be on your own someday, when you may live as you choose.

• **If your dual identity disturbs you, and you feel that your interfaith parents haven't a clue as to what you're talking about, you may very well be right!** If your parents don't understand that you have "two halves," divided loyalties, and a very different world view from theirs, bear in mind that while they survived adolescence, it wasn't from your vantage point, unless one of them is also a child of intermarriage.

• **Seek help, if your home is troubled.** If your interfaith parents, siblings, or other relatives are physically, sexually, or emotionally abusive toward you, or if they have problems with alcohol, drugs, or other compulsive behaviors, see the suggestions in chapter 8.

• **If possible, try to get to know your grandparents and other relatives in their own homes as well as in yours.** If they practice a different religion from yours, respect it, and try to learn something about it. However, it is not necessary to promise them that you'll convert to their way of life, however happy this might make them. If your parents have told you that you may choose your religion "when you grow up," consider that your teen years may be too early to make such an important determination, as a number of our respondents suggested. If you're ready, fine. But even if your grandmother feels that she'll earn spiritual brownie points by convincing you to accept Jesus or take a dunk in the *mikveh*, it is inappropriate for her to pressure you unduly. It's *your* decision, not hers. And not your parents', either.

• **Realize that all parents, regardless of their backgrounds, feel guilty about *some* aspect of their children's upbringing.** Although they may not have discussed it openly, interfaith parents often are acutely aware that their marriage has created identity problems for their children. Not knowing how to deal with these conflicts, they tend to deny that they exist.

That seemed to be the case with teenage Aviva, whom Robin met while participating in a Montreal radio talk show on the topic of the children of intermarriage. Flanked protectively by her Jewish mother and the family's rabbi, Aviva said scarcely a word throughout the program. Her mother and the rabbi volubly assured the radio audience that since Aviva had been raised as a "real" Jew, she had no unresolved identity dilemmas whatsoever, unlike those misfit descendants of intermarriage (represented by Robin) who evidently hadn't been brought up properly.

Finally the moderator asked Aviva if she was happy. The young woman paused before answering in a tiny, nervous voice, "Oh, yes, I'm perfectly happy. I identify as a Jew. There are no problems."

Would she date Christian boys as well as Jewish ones, then? After an even longer silence, she replied, "Yes. My father is Catholic, after all. But I would raise my children as Jews." Aviva's mother and the rabbi hastily broke in to proclaim that children of intermarriage brought up without any contact with Christianity would always be securely Jewish.

We often wonder what happened to poor Aviva, whose love for her father evidently made it acceptable for her to explore her "other half" by interdating. And we marvel at the loving blindness of her mother, who had followed her own heart to marry out of the faith she cherished, yet could not accept the possibility that her daughter might do the same thing.

Like other adolescent children of intermarriage, Aviva has embarked upon a journey of self-discovery, in which she'll try on new identities for size and see what fits her best. As many of the stories in the next chapter indicate, this process of discovery can last a lifetime.

CHAPTER

4

Spirituality and Ethnicity—
How We Pledge Allegiance

I feel culturally and intellectually Jewish, but spiritually and religiously Catholic. It's a fine line that I walk.
—BETTY, TEACHER

When my father learned that I'd decided to live as a Jew, he said, "I'm delighted, but don't tell your mother I said that."
—VICTORIA, PRINTING EXECUTIVE

I identify strongly with both Catholic and Jewish issues, anecdotes, and experiences on an emotional level. . . . However, I am clearly and strongly a Catholic, and I state this if needed.
—THOMAS, MANAGEMENT CONSULTANT

ONE DECEMBER DAY, LESLIE'S YOUNGER SISTER CALLED, AND was she ever aggravated. Even her voice sounded damp as she told of how torrential rain had flooded her garage and soaked her belongings, including a box of holiday decorations. "*All* the lights, *all* the ornaments," she mourned. "And when my Christmas stocking got wet, the colors ran. It's ruined. Great timing, huh?"

"What a shame, Keli," I sympathized. "Listen, I've still got my stocking around here somewhere. I've been meaning to give it to you anyway. I'll dig it out and send it."

"Naw, I can't take it," she said, genuinely shocked. She paused. "Even if I always did think your stocking was the prettiest."

"It would make me very happy to know you were enjoying it, since I don't celebrate Christmas," I told her.

"But what about when you have kids? Won't you want to hang it up for them someday?" she persisted.

"Read my lips, Keli!" I barked. *"I'm Jewish! I don't do Christmas!"*

She laughed, we both relaxed, and the stocking was dispatched through the mail the next day.

I told this story to the young rabbi with whom I was then preparing for conversion. Although he chuckled, by the way his eyes widened with disbelief at this story, as well as others pertaining to my dual heritage, he was clearly uneasy with the situation. From the remarks he'd made as we'd studied together, it was evident that like many other "born" Jews, the rabbi found it difficult to comprehend how someone as doggedly, knowledgeably Jewish as I am could remain on easy speaking terms with some of my Gentile relatives and the non-Jewish vestiges of my early life without feeling that these ties compromised my Jewishness.

Accustomed to counseling potential Jews-by-choice with two born-Gentile parents, this rabbi viewed spiritual identity as an either/or proposition. Under Jewish law, and in the minds of many Jews, the category "half-Jewish" does not exist; an individual can be only 100 percent Jewish or 100 percent Gentile. Since conversion is widely believed to be a "magic bullet," appearing before a *bet din* (rabbinic court), immersing oneself in the *mikveh*, and assuming a Hebrew name must necessarily lead to a magical transformation. Zap! You're a Jew! And nothing that came before matters.

Ironically, what I've perceived as one of the largest liabilities in my life—a lack of strong family ties and traditions—has proved to be an asset in my final choice of spiritual identity. Many other descendants of intermarriage say that they are so torn by their fierce, loving allegiances to both of their worlds that they've found it difficult or impossible to settle primarily in one.

Deciding where we belong spiritually, ethnically, and culturally remains one of the most excruciating tasks that we encounter, say a number of the adult children and grandchildren of intermarriage. Some make a selection early in life and stick to it. Some try on different spiritual identities for size, year after year, group after group, leaving the discards in a heap on the closet floor. And some descendants of intermarriage we've queried have remained permanently undecided, locked in painful stasis between their two worlds, immobilized by conflicting loyalties.

Others, reluctant to reject either parent's world, pledge allegiance to both Judaism and Christianity, often by jumbling together very different traditions and values, like an overambitious and not entirely palatable turkey stuffing. Or they select a third path, which they may claim is unrelated either to Judaism or to Christianity, whether or not it actually is.

During the past few years we have talked with hundreds of descendants of intermarriage. We originally estimated that half of the individuals we informally interviewed live as Jews, a quarter as Christians, and the remainder are religiously unaffiliated or follow a "third path." Those ballpark figures were approximated by the questionnaires completed for this book: 44 percent of our respondents identify as Jews, 29 percent as Christians, and 27 percent consider themselves "nothing," "both," follow a "third path," or profess no particular spiritual identity.

Searching for labels. Within certain boundaries, we let our respondents tell us which category they belong to. Although Jewish law defines all children of a Jewish mother or maternal grandmother as Jews (unless they've formally converted to another religion, and even then, they remain ethnically Jewish), we classified our respondents as Jews,

Christians, or "other" in accordance with the choices *they themselves have made.*

Forty-four percent of our respondents state unambiguously that they are Jewish. We did *not* limit membership in this group to those with Jewish mothers who were raised as Jews and to patrilineal descendants of intermarriage who have converted to Judaism. (If the respondents said they were Jewish, that was good enough for us.) Of our matrilineal respondents, just 52 percent identify as Jews. This finding vigorously challenges one of the most pervasive myths cherished by the Jewish community—that the children of Jewish women and Gentile men will always identify unambiguously as the "real" Jews they're supposed to be.

Most matrilineal descendants of intermarriage concede that their halachically correct status gives them a running start toward the goal of a "real" Jewish life. However, if the adult child of a Jewish woman and Gentile man opts for Christianity, this decision may provoke more enmity from the Jewish community than might a similar decision by a patrilineal. Since matrilineal descendants are generally considered "real" Jews, their adoption of Christianity is more likely to be seen as a traitorous defection by "born" Jews.

Christian-identified respondents, who comprise 29 percent of the total, include individuals with Jewish fathers *or* Jewish mothers who have actively chosen a Christian way of life. Among the Christians, we have assembled members of traditional denominations such as Catholicism, Methodism, and Lutheranism, as well as adherents of quasi-Christian positive-thought groups, such as the Church of Religious Science. This category also embraces "Hebrew Christians" and Messianic Jews, Unitarians, and Quakers, for reasons we'll explore later in this chapter.

If someone terms himself an "agnostic nothing," yet has a Jewish mother, *halacha* would deem that person a Jew. Yet we've placed him among the 27 percent of our respondents who say that they are "nothing," "half and half," identify most strongly with their non-Jewish ethnic background, or have opted for a non-Christian or non-Jewish belief structure. This remarkably diverse group also includes individuals whose loyalties are split many ways, with no one ethnicity predominating, as with one Canadian respondent who says he's "Jewish/Christian/American Indian."

Most descendants of intermarriage *hate* being forced into a mold, and those who felt drawn to specify their allegiances to the letter made tabulating the data just a little more complicated. One man, for example, says he's a "religious Roman Catholic/ethnic Zionist Jew." Where does he belong, at least for statistical purposes? (We counted him among the Christians, but hate to see the Jewish community dismiss him as irrelevant, as this guy clearly loves his Jewish "half"!) Many others struggle visibly to find a category into which they can comfortably fit. "I call myself 'nothing,' or 'Russian,' " says one woman. "Greek mind, Jewish heart," says another, while a third notes, "I'm a conglomerate. If pressed for something more specific, I'm officially Presbyterian."

Humor also plays a part as we search for a label that accurately summarizes our contents. One matrilineal respondent who actually is quite committed to his Reform Jewish congregation quips that he's a "recovering Jew," while his brother is an ordained Baptist minister. Another man waggishly remarks that he's a "semi-Semitic Jewish hillbilly."

As descendants of intermarriage ourselves, we know how hard it can be to answer that deceptively simple question: "What *are* you, anyway?" Those who were raised by two Jewish or two Christian parents—"bornies," we call 'em— often cringe at our efforts to name ourselves. Most "bornies" show scant understanding of what it's like to have two distinctly different parental cultures vie for our attention. "Coming from a mixed marriage made me desire to belong to or identify with something strongly," says Carla, who was raised in a secular home. She now affiliates with the Roman Catholicism that her father abandoned, but remains close to her Jewish mother's relatives.

Our need to determine as well as maintain a religious and ethnic identity is one of the major issues that sets the descendants of intermarriage apart from our friends and relatives who have two Jewish or two Gentile parents. Roman Catholics, baptized as infants, or Jews raised by two Orthodox parents, will usually cherish their identity and tend to perceive it as their birthright, rather than as something that they had a hand in deciding. For "free-thinkers" from endogamous homes for whom organized religion means nothing, our split allegiances may appear not only unnecessary but laughable. "I never go to synagogue myself, but that doesn't matter," a secular Jewish woman once told us. "Judaism is transmitted culturally, and religion really isn't a part of it, for me. As far as I'm concerned, you children of intermarriage are all *goyim* [non-Jews]."

More tactful "bornies" may simply fail to understand why spiritual and ethnic identity matters so much to so many adult children and grandchildren of intermarriage. "What difference does it make what you call yourselves?" they ask us.

A lot. And unfortunately, there are few, if any, easy answers to our identity questions. It's tempting to daydream about how our concerns would be more easily addressed if *something* about our backgrounds could change. These "solution fantasies" include:

- If my interfaith parents had raised me in no religion (as a Jew, as a Christian), I wouldn't have "two halves."

- If I convert to Judaism, I'll be totally accepted by "born" Jews, and my Gentile "half" will vanish.
- If I become a Christian, my Jewish "half" will disappear, and anti-Semitism needn't concern me.
- If I align with a liberal, undogmatic version of Christianity, such as Unitarianism or Quakerism, I won't be a "real" Christian. That might allow me to keep both my "halves" without any conflict.
- If I adopt a third, unrelated path, such as Buddhism or Islam, I'll be free of my "two worlds."
- If I just give up on both of my parents' religions and all ethnic ties, I'll have no more conflicts.

Descendants of intermarriage indulge in all of these fantasies, and more. That's because we come—will always come—from two specific worlds. Nothing can change that. And unfortunately, neither the Jewish nor the Gentile community knows quite what to do with us. We must help ourselves, and one another.

As we discussed in chapter 3, a battle rages in the Jewish community over the question, "Who is a Jew?" Anti-Semitism or a strong desire to accommodate their Jewish "half" as well may keep descendants of intermarriage from feeling comfortable within the Christian world. A third path, such as Hindu-influenced mysticism and meditation, or a completely secular life, may not satisfy our longings for a sense of connection with our past, of belonging to both of our "halves" without sacrificing either, and without compromising the often-conflicting membership requirements of Judaism and Christianity.

Reconciling our duality can be such an arduous process that 53 percent of our respondents concede that it has been difficult or impossible to find a spiritual home in which to settle, even if they identify as Jews or Christians. Many say, as Bernard does, that their communal ties remain fluid and undefined. Raised in his mother's Roman Catholic faith, Bernard notes that rather than living between two worlds, "what I feel is a *lack*. A lack of belonging. What is my heritage? Catholicism? I don't believe in it. Judaism? I hardly speak English."

Bernard speaks movingly of his split allegiances, rather than insisting that his duality does not exist, as often happens among members of interfaith families. He also was fortunate to grow up with parents who acknowledged their religious and ethnic differences. However, their personal sense of rightful placement in their respective cultures did not extend to their children, says Bernard, adding that his parents cannot see his confusion as an inevitable by-product of their family dynamics. Now married to a Jewish-identified woman who is also a descendant of intermarriage, Bernard thinks of himself as a Jew. Yet he is keenly aware of the inadequacy of his Jewish education, which he feels bars him from fuller participation in Jewish activities.

Whether we decide at the age of five or fifty, most descendants of intermarriage do eventually align themselves with a primary or blended spiritual and ethnic identity, even if they call themselves "nothing." Some of those who identify with no particular group do so rather sourly, as does Parker, who says he has "no religious affiliation. I hated [Unitarian] Sunday school, and I wanted to be an atheist when I grew up. I lead a secular life, steering clear of both Christian and Jewish religions."

Unlike Parker, who prefers to think of himself as having "no halves," 54 percent of our respondents replied affirmatively to the question, "Do you ever feel as if you have 'two halves' existing within you?" Whether they replied "yes" or "no," virtually everyone had an interesting explanation. For example:

- "Yes, I'm like the Soviet Union, which is neither an Asian nation nor a European nation, but both," says a man with a Jewish mother, an agnostic Protestant father, and no current religious affiliation.
- "Yes, but I feel more like I have a shadow self—my Jewish heritage," says a woman with a Jewish father who was raised in her mother's Catholic faith.
- "Yes, that's true. I'm very lucky to be part of two worlds! I got twice as much heritage and more than twice as much life—*and I love it!*" bubbles the daughter of a Jewish man and a Christian woman.
- "No, just one whole with a lot of extra benefits," says a man with a Jewish mother and a Catholic-reared father who was raised in the Jewish community and remains there today, although his sister converted to Episcopalianism.
- "Yes, that is the most logical solution for me. I feel loyal to both traditions," notes a daughter of a Protestant woman and Jewish man, adding, "I was raised Christian, married a Jew, and my sons had *bar mitzvahs.* I don't know what to call myself."
- "More like twenty facets," says a woman whose Catholic mother converted to Judaism.
- "Two halves? That's putting it mildly! I have felt like a schizophrenic for most of my life! Or perhaps a giant piece of taffy, constantly being stretched and pulled to capacity in both directions. . . . For as long as I can remember, I have yearned to integrate, or magically fuse, my two halves, so I wouldn't have to choose one over the other. It has always been a source of irritation, frustration, and great sadness that the two are regarded as mutually exclusive by many," says an Episcopalian-educated woman, daughter of an Orthodox Jewish woman and a Christian man.
- "Yes, definitely two halves. I feel that part of me screams out for recognition and a place to truly belong and feel

accepted," says a Christian-identified daughter of a Jewish man and an Episcopalian woman. Her husband, also Christian, and the son of a Jewish woman and a Presbyterian man, adds, "Because the Jewish and Christian communities themselves are so polarized, I am just a reflection of this."

- "No, I didn't feel I belonged either place," says a daughter of a Jewish man and a Christian woman, adding, "You see, I never had two clear halves. . . . With Jews, I tend to want to simply be known as Jewish, no explanations, because I have made a choice, feel Jewish, and like the sense of belonging. With Christians, I'm more apt to share my history in order to identify with them and belong there also."
- "Yes. I am training myself to live in one world, without forgetting that I have a second half," remarks a daughter of a Jewish woman and a Catholic-raised man, who during her college years chose to identify as Jewish.
- "No, but I have the best of both worlds—Jewish above the neck and Italian below the waist," wisecracks the son of a Jewish man and Catholic woman.

And when asked whether they felt they had "two halves," several people answered cryptically, "Yes *and* no." How Zen! And what telling evidence of our duality!

However, even if we are able to find a toehold in one religious and ethnic culture, our quest for identity does not end. While we establish our rights to membership in our chosen group, we must find honorable ways to maintain the ties that will always bind us to our "other half."

One of the most compelling obligations we face is acknowledging and respecting the feelings of our relatives without shortchanging our own needs. If we remain in the culture in which we were raised, the parent and relatives who "lost" us at birth eventually come to realize that we may never switch allegiances and perpetuate their heritage. If we have left the milieu in which we were raised, even if we were brought up "as nothing," at least one of our parents, and other relatives as well, is likely to feel that we have defied his or her wishes, whether privately held or forcefully expressed.

Start spreading the news. When Jason Bernstein, son of two Jewish parents, comes home from Oberlin to announce that he's become a disciple of the International Society for Krishna Consciousness, it is practically a given that his mother will faint, his father will rant, and the phone bills will soar as this succulent bit of gossip makes its way around. If Deirdre Carmody becomes a Jew-by-choice, her Roman Catholic parents will worry over where her soul will spend eternity. Yet, most people we've talked to—excluding the descendants of intermarriage, who know better—assume that *interfaith* parents always take their children's spiritual and ethnic wanderings in stride, especially if they've assured their children that the choice is theirs to make in adulthood.

In fact, breaking the news to one's interfaith parents and grandparents may touch off a firestorm of protest that feels like an unpleasant extension of adolescent rebellion. Some descendants of intermarriage postpone announcing their decisions to their families for as long as possible, even indefinitely. "I wish I could find the courage to reveal my faith to my wife and parents," laments Douglas, the son of an Orthodox-reared Jewish man and a Catholic woman of Portuguese-Irish descent. "I consider myself a Jewish Christian, since I accepted Jesus Christ as my personal Savior but I have no experience attending either a church or a synagogue," he says. Douglas worships privately, through nightly prayer.

Announcing one's primary allegiance may, in fact, deeply wound all of the parties involved. "The worst part of interfaith marriages is that when the child decides on one religion it necessarily means rejecting the faith or heritage of one parent. This hurts both parent and child," explains Bethany, a housewife who also operates a home-based business. The daughter of a "secular humanist" Gentile man and a woman who was raised in an Orthodox Jewish home, Bethany embraced evangelical Christianity after her parents divorced during her teenage years.

Even her father is "very negative" about her spiritual path, she says, explaining that he objects not to her Christianity but to her fervor. "He would prefer that I weren't too radical. He doesn't like it that I spend so much time and effort on things of a religious nature," notes Bethany, who makes a special effort to "share the Gospel" with others, and attends church services and Bible-study sessions regularly. Her mother reacted even more vehemently. Remarks Bethany:

> When I first became a Christian, my mother thought it was a phase. When she realized it was not, she panicked, and pretty much disowned me. She didn't want to have anything to do with me. Every time we spoke, it was an argument.
>
> My mother thought I had been brainwashed, and harassed me. She sent me to many Jewish people, including her relatives, to try to win me back. The final showdown came when I was engaged to be married. My mom knew that if I married a Christian, which I did, that would be *it*. She had no intention of coming to our wedding, but decided only the night before that she would attend.
>
> Since then, she has accepted my husband and the fact that we are Christians. However, she doesn't like it one bit.

Validating Mom and Dad. As we'll discuss in chapter 5, when adult descendants of intermarriage choose mates and bear children, these major life changes tend to strengthen our spiritual and identity choices. If we've previously coasted along undecided, upon marrying or becoming a parent we may feel a dawning sense of urgency to settle on a particular way of life, in order to practice the religious and cultural rituals that will enrich our new homes and families. However we decide, our own parents' influence remains strong. In turn, our life choices have a powerful impact upon them.

We have heard myriad descriptions of the ways—directly, obliquely, harshly, poignantly—in which interfaith parents and grandparents have expressed their craving for approval both from their families and from society. Even today, most interfaith couples cannot expect to bask in the same sort of uncritical praise and affirmation that endogamous brides and grooms usually enjoy. Stung by years of trying to rationalize their right to marry in the first place, interfaith couples may look to their children—tangible evidence of their love—to validate their decision to "marry out." Consciously or un-consciously, intermarried parents may feel that the surest form of approval is for their offspring to select the culture or religion in which they raised them, or to reject the cultures that they themselves discarded.

At times, a parent or grandparent is quietly elated to see an offspring adopt his or her former loyalties. However, in our experience, such cases are outnumbered by scenarios in which an intermarried parent or grandparent, hungry for support, makes it clear that a descendant who opts for a different path might just as well change his or her name to Benedict Arnold.

"My [Mormon] mother displays overt hostility about my identity as a Jew," says Linda, an attorney for the federal government. She adds that her mother's disapproval spills over into other parts of her life as well, noting dryly, "Mom feels I should be practicing law in the private sector, earning lots of money. She mentions it frequently."

If their nuptial vows served as a passport to a radically

new way of life, a partner in an interfaith marriage may be openly dismayed and puzzled by what he or she views as an adult child's atavistic desire to reclaim ground that the parent has relinquished. "My [Jewish] mother doesn't comprehend my desire to be Jewish, as she desperately tries to hold on to the Gentile world she had when she was married to my [Christian] father," remarks Jessica.

Descendants of intermarriage frequently tell us that their interfaith parents, like people from same-faith homes, simply don't understand why identity looms so large in their lives. As we discussed in chapter 2, many interfaith couples cheerfully, though inaccurately, assert that since their bicultural status is "no big deal" for them, their children will just naturally feel the same way. Others raise their children in a particular parental culture with the expectation that as adults, their offspring will obediently remain there—*all* of them.

Although we may yearn to please *both* of our interfaith parents by our choice of religious and ethnic identity, the mixed signals we receive from our two families make this very difficult. In addition, through their decision to marry cross-culturally, interfaith couples have forfeited any right to dictate their adult children's and grandchildren's ultimate allegiances. (It's debatable whether even same-faith parents enjoy such a privilege!) Judging from the experiences of the hundreds of descendants of intermarriage we've studied, interfaith parents appear to have no guarantees—*none at all*—that as adults their offspring will follow the path chosen for them, no matter how they were raised.

This lack of certainty extends across the spectrum of interfaith families, from one-religion-only homes to "no big deal" households in which the children have been told that they can choose for themselves when they grow up. Often, when interfaith parents who are secular free spirits grant this permission, they assume that their kids will opt to emulate them by following no particular spiritual path or group affiliation. "My parents would not have been pleased if I'd chosen Judaism *or* Christianity," says Leigh, who was raised in a secular home. "My mother used to say, 'Jews are fanatics, but Christians are *tacky*.' " Today, Leigh lives as a Jew, one of her siblings is a born-again Christian, and the other espouses no faith.

My brother's druthers. The inherent duality of interfaith families lives on in the ultimate religious choices of their offspring. Of the individuals formally surveyed for this book, just 26 percent said that all of their siblings shared their religious identity, or lack thereof; in at least half of those cases, all of the siblings considered themselves agnostics, atheists, secular Jews, or secular Christians. A whopping 57 percent said that their brothers and sisters followed spiritual paths that were not at all congruent with their own. For example, Arnie, son of a Protestant woman and Jewish man, notes, "I call myself Jewish or pantheistic, depending on who is asking. My older sister says she's 'mixed,' while my younger brother is a Rastafarian."

The remaining 17 percent of our respondents are "only" children, or don't know what their siblings believe. Many are no more than vaguely aware of their brothers' and sisters' affiliations, confessing, "It isn't anything we're comfortable bringing up," or, "We have a tacit agreement not to discuss my Jewishness and his atheism," or, "Our family thought it 'wasn't nice' to talk about religion."

Other respondents guessed wrong when providing their siblings' affiliations. Several respondents stated clearly that a brother or sister espoused a particular faith. Yet, when we received that sibling's questionnaire, he or she said something entirely different. Even among relatives who converse freely, it may not be easy to describe what motivates us to select a particular identity. "My sister is confused that I have chosen one religion over another, as she still considers herself half and half," notes Jewish-identified Jessica.

By virtue of its unusual size, Marnie's family provides a vivid panorama of the spiritual destinies that may be pursued by the children of interfaith parents. She relates:

> My mother's religion is Jewish, and ethnically she's just plain American. My father is Polish and Catholic. They separated after thirty years of marriage due to these differences. I was raised secularly with a smattering of Catholicism from my Catholic grandmother, and a brief after-school religious-ed course until I was about eleven. I took this quite seriously. . . .
>
> I'm the oldest of ten children. Two brothers have their own type of humanistic religion and believe in a Supreme Being. One brother calls himself agnostic. One brother is a Messianic Jew. Two brothers call themselves Catholic, but practice minimally. One brother identifies as a fundamentalist Christian religiously but is a Zionist Jew ethically. Two sisters call themselves Jewish but feel "American."

"The family Jew." By the examples they set, siblings who affiliate differently effectively smash common stereotypes about how the offspring of interfaith families are "supposed to" affiliate and feel. For instance, a descendant of intermarriage may joke about being considered the "family Jew"—regardless of his actual affiliation—because of the intensity of his personality and his facial features. Or perhaps the "family Jew" is the child whose personality reflects "Jewish" tastes and interests, preferring horseradish to mayonnaise, playing chess rather than ice hockey, majoring in accounting instead of agronomy.

Popular mythology describing interfaith families contends

that the "family Jew" or the "blond *shiksa* [Gentile female]" will necessarily affiliate with the religious and ethnic identity that they superficially resemble. However, many descendants of intermarriage don't fit these molds, and may strenuously reject being forced into them.

Meg and Patty, the daughters of a Jewish Holocaust survivor and his Christian wife, chafe at their status as halachically non-Jewish; they and one of their brothers have formally converted to Judaism or plan to do so in the near future. "It's funny that our other brother, who is not affiliated with any religion, is the most argumentative and reactive and defensive in discussing the issue. Also, he is the 'most Jewish' in character and personality. I *hate* being told this!" Patty says ruefully.

Conversely, a descendant of intermarriage who's opted to live as a Jew yet doesn't "look Jewish" is more likely to see the legitimacy of his or her spiritual claim challenged. "My demeanor mirrors my father's and my father's mother's—WASPy and aloof, with a good deal of Jewish emotion thrown in. I also look like my dad, who is blond, green-eyed, and fair," notes Jessica, a Jewish-identified woman who says that Jews often express disbelief that she is "one of them," despite her mother's status as a "born" Jew.

Amid the myriad reasons the adult children of intermarriage give for their religious and spiritual choices, certain themes emerge for each option. Imagine, for a moment, that our interfaith parents' heritages fuse to emit a single steady beam of white light. Once we reach adulthood, that beam shines through the prism that we and our siblings form. Thus refracted, the light explodes into the entire rainbow spectrum of the religious and ethnic cultures we carry within. Which colors will predominate in our lives?

Living out our Jewish "half." A wide variety of reasons was given by the 44 percent of our respondents who have chosen to live as Jews. Some commonly sounded themes include:

• **"I've never considered myself anything but Jewish, even when other Jews disagreed."** Being Jewish is a volitional state for the adult children of intermarriage, whether our status is matrilineal or patrilineal. The concept of Jewishness as an *option* rather than as a *given* sticks in the craw of many "born" Jews, although it applies, in truth, to anyone with one *or* two Jewish parents who lives in a democratic, pluralistic society. Yet, when the descendants of intermarriage choose Judaism, we can never quite take our status for granted, however observant our lives or halachically correct our status may be.

If we are patrilineal, raised in a non-Jewish religious culture, or have not converted to Judaism under Orthodox auspices, some "born" Jews consider us Gentile. Consequently, if we identify as Jews, we may try to say as little as possible about our backgrounds and hope that nobody asks. It is fairly easy for a patrilineal to "pass" in Jewish circles, at least initially, if he or she bears, courtesy of a Jewish father or grandfather, a stereotypically Jewish name, such as Goldberg, Katz, or Berkowitz, or one that is ethnically neutral and common to Jews who have Anglicized their names, such as Harris, Green, or Cole.

"Though a lot of people think I shouldn't consider myself Jewish, I believe I am," argues Rachel, whose surname is unambiguously Jewish. Raised as a Methodist, she now worships in a Conservative synagogue. She stresses, "I feel strongly about the fact that because my mom isn't Jewish, I shouldn't be considered so. It should be whatever is in your heart."

Even some matrilineal descendants of intermarriage—the so-called "real" Jews—maintain a more precarious position in the Jewish community than many "bornies" realize. At first glance, our typically non-Jewish surnames may give us away, forcing us to get bogged down in tiresome explanations. *Halacha* notwithstanding, a surprising number of "born" Jews say that having a Gentile father dilutes the full measure of Jewish status that a matrilineal descendant of intermarriage supposedly enjoys. In addition, both matrilineals and patrilineals find that "born" Jews who are uncomfortable with our status tend to shrug off our emotional ties to our Gentile parents or grandparents as irrelevant both religiously and ethnically.

In our wary defensiveness, both matrilineals and patrilineals are likely to envy the self-confidence that "born" Jews exhibit about their identity. We may also privately deplore the lack of commitment that some of them demonstrate toward their heritage. Moreover, our presence in the Jewish community tends to discomfit those who feel negative about their own Jewishness. A number of Jewish-identified descendants of intermarriage report that their co-religionists have asked bluntly, "Why on earth would anyone choose to be Jewish if they had the option *not* to?" One particularly compelling answer follows.

• **"I felt the Jews needed me more."** Keenly aware that Jews have been underdogs throughout their history, and that their ranks were cruelly decimated by the Holocaust, Jewish-identified descendants of intermarriage frequently say that they are voting with their hearts as well as their feet.

• **"I just can't accept Christianity. The religious tenets of Judaism make more sense to me."** These descendants report that they are strongly drawn by Jewish theology, mysticism, religious law, and ritual, and while they respect their Gentile heritage, they usually reject Christ's divinity and the concept of his death upon the cross for redemptive reasons. "I feel Jesus was a remarkable man, but not my Lord, and I certainly don't pray to my Lord through him. God is God. I also feel comfortable with the theological precepts of liberal Judaism," says Shira, who was raised in an "agnostic, eclectic" home with exposure to both Jewish and Christian customs and beliefs, and chose Reform Judaism as an adult.

• **"I consider myself a secular Jew."** Descendants of inter-marriage who display this perspective may not be willing or able to live a religiously observant life, but still wish to carry on some of the traditions of relatives who modeled the sec-ular Jewish behavior common in the United States. Descen-dants of intermarriage who follow this path are unabashed bagels-and-lox Jews. Their loyalties are reflected in their love of Jewish culture, food, music, and certain home-based rit-uals, such as lighting a Hanukkah *menorah* or staging a Pass-over *seder*, and by their involvement in Jewish communal organizations and causes.

• **"Judaism reached out and grabbed me."** Intense ethnic or spiritual experiences virtually compelled some descen-dants of intermarriage to become Jews, and may account in part for the fact that although just 17 percent of our respon-dents were raised as Jews, 44 percent affiliate that way today. Adoptees may feel a strong yearning toward Judaism upon learning that a birth parent was Jewish. Others were trig-gered by a deeply moving event, such as a trip to Israel, an exciting introductory class in Hebrew or Jewish history, or the discovery that a parent or grandparent was a "runaway" or left his or her birth culture under pressure (usually by converting from Judaism to Christianity), a concept we'll explore in greater detail in chapter 8. Such an experience may result in an instantaneous commitment to Judaism, or at the very least to a strong desire to learn more about their other "half."

Living out our Christian "half." Twenty-nine percent of those we surveyed formally say that they live as Christians. Although the two religious traditions are obviously not the same, many of the reasons given for choosing Christianity closely resemble the responses from the Jewish-identified respondents. It's as if the same puzzle pieces that make up a bicultural family can be fitted together to yield either a Christian or a Jewish child, without a scrap left over.

• **"I grew up in a Christian neighborhood, so I sort of went with the flow."** Many Christian descendants of intermarriage end up identifying with America's majority culture because it's all around them—easy to see, easy to join. "I was free to choose my own religious affiliation as a child," says Cindy. "Since I had greater access to Protestant churches, I attended them much more frequently than synagogues." After her parents divorced when she was four, she lived with her Presbyterian mother. "I think my proximity to Christian institutions, organizations, and people has been the main factor in deciding to be a Christian. I never seriously considered converting to Judaism."

Nevertheless, adds Cindy, "It has been difficult for me to find a spiritual home, as I am always questioning my beliefs. Only once, when I was active with conservative Christians, did I find spiritual affiliation easy, and that was because I turned off my brain." Cindy, who bears her father's unequivocally Jewish surname, says that she definitely feels her duality. "I have squelched my Jewish half, and it sometimes saddens me," she says.

The concept of accepting one's faith as an act of free will is more familiar to Christians than to Jews, for although one can be born Gentile, one must actively *choose* Christianity. Despite the Christian culture's emphasis on self-determination, and its acceptance of converts, Christian-identified children of intermarriage are often stung by Christian anti-Semitism, as well as by the negative response of Jews who chide them for abandoning their "Jewish half." Candace, who is Catholic, remarks, "Christian adult children of intermarriage like myself are often considered traitors by the Jewish community, just like 'full' Jews who convert to Christianity. This constitutes a double-whammy since the Jewish community generally ostracizes us as 'not really Jewish' in the first place."

• **"I never felt that the Jews wanted me."** The Jewish community's discomfort with the children of intermarriage was felt sharply by Irwin. Now nearly seventy years old, he was expelled from Hebrew school at his parents' synagogue "at the age of five or six, when they found out my mother was Gentile," he recalls. When he was thirteen, Irwin was baptized as a Christian. All his life, he says, he's shopped around religiously, dabbling in "Christianity, yoga, and Zen Buddhism." About his status as a child of intermarriage, Irwin says, "I don't recall ever hearing a positive comment," yet he is still considering converting to Judaism. Spiritually, Irwin says he feels "isolation mostly, some sadness, and a sense of loss."

Jewish animosity toward her ambiguous status was one of the factors that prompted Betty to turn away from the secular Jewish culture in which she was raised. The biological daughter of a Jewish man and a Gentile woman, who placed her for adoption with a secular Jewish couple, Betty has been enthusiastically participating in Catholic ritual for more than a decade. "However, even ten years after my conversion, I'm still not sure what to do about my recurring Jewishness," Betty reflects. "One thing puzzles me about *being* Jewish, though. Why would anyone want to be part of a community that doesn't welcome us as we are for who we are?"

• **"Christians made me feel so much at home that it was only a short step to accepting Jesus Christ as my Savior."** After nearly two thousand years of missionary efforts, Christianity is well positioned to welcome the descendants of Jewish-Gentile intermarriage—generically, if not specifically. Unlike the Jewish community's many outreach organizations, the Christian community makes no particular effort to woo interfaith families. However, one reason that Christian groups don't bother specifically targeting Jewish-Gentile couples is that it's not really necessary to do so. Every church, however poorly organized or lukewarm in its outreach, is dedicated to finding, teaching, and converting newcomers of any ethnic background.

Judaism ceased to be a missionary religion in the centuries that followed the adoption of Christianity as the official religion of the Roman Empire and its successor states. Christian laws against Jewish-Christian intermarriage and punitive—even bloody—Christian reprisals against communities that accepted converts to Judaism convinced Jewish leaders that missionary work was too costly. Jews came to shun proselytizing, concentrating instead on *tikkun olam* (the transformation and repair of the world) through the efforts of "born" Jews and of Jews-by-choice who find their way into Judaism on their own. Conversely, followers of both Christianity and Islam are intent upon converting the world, of reaching nonbelievers and tenuously committed members of their own faiths alike.

Those descendants of intermarriage who are living out their Christian "halves" say that they felt warmly welcomed by churches who valued their membership. They praise Christian universality and the notion that God seeks persons of all backgrounds to accept Christ. Descendants of intermarriage who have happily chosen Christianity say that their spiritual quest has met with the sympathy and assistance that they could not find elsewhere. "I decided on Christianity because I saw more positive attributes in the good Christians I knew than in the good Jews I knew. And the story of Christ's life and death and resurrection sounds so *right* to me, I want to believe in it," explains Jacob, a son of a Jewish woman and a Presbyterian man.

Among the Christian denominations, descendants of interfaith couples appear particularly drawn to the Unitarian Church, which is perceived by many as more deistic and focused upon ethics than specifically "Christian" in philosophy. Quakerism also appeals, with its emphasis on silent prayer and connection to an individual's inner "light of God," rather than invoking God through a church hierarchy and sacraments.

Joyce is one adult child of intermarriage who feels a strong sense of relief at how Unitarianism allowed her to balance her "halves":

> The Unitarian Church offers me a place in which one aspect of my heritage need not cancel out the other. I always experienced institutionalized Christianity as a double-edged sword; it promised comfort, solace, and belonging, but these were not available unconditionally. It's lovely to hear, "Come unto me, all ye that labor and are heavy laden, and I will give you rest."
>
> However, in the next breath comes the admonition, "No one comes to the Father except by me." I was touched by the beckoning, comforting words of Christianity and then jolted to feel the door slammed in my face by verses specifying just who would receive God's grace. I couldn't understand a religion that embraced half my family and rejected the rest. It seemed to me that it might find half of me acceptable and the other half destined for condemnation.
>
> I was attracted by the breadth of religious thought and expression that exists in the Unitarian Church. I am grateful to have found a place of worship in which I can feel comfortable.

Other Christian descendants of intermarriage have told us that their mixed status is actually an asset in their religious communities. A member of the Church of Jesus Christ of the Latter-day Saints remarks, "Mormons have always reacted positively to my background. After all, Jews are children of Israel, and therefore a chosen people." Adds a Seventh-Day Adventist, "My knowledge of the Jewish Sabbath made it easier for me to understand the seventh-day Sabbath that Adventists believe in."

Edward speaks for many Christian-identified descendants of intermarriage when he explains, "My dual exposure to both faiths has deepened my understanding and provided broad-based insights." A Holocaust survivor and the son of a Jewish woman and a Christian man, Edward calls himself an Episcopalian, but notes that he does, indeed, have "two halves." They have provided "an enriching experience, not without pain, but a greatly maturing process," he says.

As we've previously stated, it would be grossly unfair to categorize the adult descendants of intermarriage as forever caught between the rock and the hard place of their Jewish and Christian "halves." A number have indicated that their status is genuinely "no big deal" and actually can be an enrichment to their lives. Even so, some say that their duality provides an ongoing sense of dislocation and a difficulty in locating places where their souls can comfortably roost.

This confusion is eloquently expressed by Kim, a Christian-raised daughter of a Jewish man and a Baptist-turned-Episcopalian woman, who apparently believes that one can be a Christian without believing in Christ:

> Deep in my heart, I believe that God knows and accepts me for who and what I am, and He knows of my great love for Him. Though I do not fit into any specific "house of faith," my relationship and bond with Him is formal. I am perfectly comfortable in church. I simply omit certain words, such as "Jesus," or "Christ the Son," in songs and prayers. I don't say what I don't believe.

Although her son attends an Episcopalian school, Kim says, "I belong to *no* organized institution or group. But I have never searched for one, since I feel no need to belong to an organized group."

Special "Christian half" problems. Kim's comments highlight a form of spiritual and ethnic confusion that we have found more frequently among descendants of intermarriage who are living out their Christian "half" than among their Jewish-identified counterparts. Typically, descendants of intermarriage who opt for Judaism or a mainstream denomination of Christianity are well aware of the theological and social implications of their choice. While continuing to care for relatives from their other "half," these committed individuals are quite certain that they are not *spiritually* part of that world. Such clarity of vision may be hard-won, but these descendants of intermarriage appear cognizant of the major spiritual and ethnic disparities that differentiate their two worlds.

While the descendants of intermarriage can—and should— find much joy and pleasure in our dual heritages, channel switching like Claire's may raise a few eyebrows. The daughter of a Jewish man and a Gentile woman of German descent, Claire was reared as a Unitarian and says she finds no conflict in her dual loyalties. "I'm Christian at Christmas. It's a lovely holiday when you ignore the crass commercialism. Besides, Christians have *great* music. And at Passover, I'm Jewish. It's another wonderful holiday with great ethical and political meaning to me," she says.

While religious cultures such as Islam can reasonably be considered "third paths," those individuals who affiliate with Christian-rooted denominations such as Unitarianism, Quakerism, the Church of Religious Science, or Messianic Judaism (e.g., Jews for Jesus) are essentially joining the Christian world.

In the interests of offering a universal welcome to newcomers, Unitarian, Quaker, and other quasi-Christian groups tend to deemphasize their Christian origins, thereby inadvertently encouraging the mistaken view that these denominations represent an alternative to both Judaism and Christianity. In the absence of traditional Christian symbolism—crucifixes, church hierarchies, sacraments, or mentions of Jesus in a redemptive capacity—some congregants may erroneously come to assume that Jesus, either as the son of God or as a revered teacher, is not a central focus.

If a descendant of intermarriage passionately desires a religion that actively combines both his parents' worlds, he or she may become involved with Jews for Jesus, whose adherents are also known as Hebrew Christians and Messianic Jews. Rather than providing a "third path," Messianic Judaism actually provides an avenue into the Christian community, as these groups' goal is to persuade as many Jews as possible to accept Jesus.

Whether "born" Jews or descendants of intermarriage, Messianic Jews tend to have "shallow Jewish backgrounds and reach adulthood with Judaism crossed off the menu as a real-life option," says Rabbi Michael Skobac, New York director of Jews for Judaism, a national countermissionary group. He adds that since prospective Hebrew Christians tend to get

> . . . choked off at the prospect of completely trashing their fragile Jewish identities and assimilating into Gentile churches, Messianic Judaism became the ideal marketing strategy to get Jewish people over the hump: "You're not converting to another religion—you're becoming a completed Jew, a more fulfilled Jew!"

We feel that it is important to be specific about this particular area of confusion, as descendants of intermarriage often are so desperate to honor both of their "halves" that they wander down a path rife with intellectual dishonesty ("I can accept Christ as Lord and *still* be a Jew"). Descendants of intermarriage who want to live as Christians should not feel obliged to profess that this deeply felt choice is a "third path." Although one never loses one's *ethnic* Jewish heritage, both our Jewish and Christian "halves" are dishonored by believing that one can claim full religious status as both an observant Jew and as a devout Christian. To do so not only violates Jewish law but conflicts with the demand, expressed throughout most of Christian history, that converts to Christianity give up *all* other religions, as well as the practices dictated by those religions.

Opting out of *any* organized spiritual setting seems to suit some individuals to a T. "I'm just not interested in formally joining any particular group," says Claire. "My seeking has been mostly in the area of ethics—how I shall live as a kind and just person in a world which is often unkind and unjust. This has mostly taken the form of late-night bull sessions and much reading." Other descendants of intermarriage cite activities that, while not specifically "religious," bring them inner peace, such as meditation, yoga, physical exercise, nurturing friendships, and "just trying to be a good person, in a manner that brings honor on both of my families," as one man put it.

The following suggestions are intended to help you ease into a spiritual world that you may comfortably call your own:

• **If you're choosing a religious and ethnic identity for the first time, examine both cultures carefully before settling on Judaism or Christianity, or rejecting them in favor of a "third path" or secular life.** Don't decide solely on the basis of negative factors: family quarrels, divorce, or parental reluctance to see you become involved in either of your heritages.

• **Don't let a lack of religious or cultural education keep you from pursuing spiritual goals.** Virtually every synagogue, church, fellowship, Quaker meeting, Zen center— you name it—offers courses for beginners. Don't be afraid to admit your ignorance. Many of your contemporaries, reared in same-faith "real" Jewish or "real" Christian homes, know as little as you might, and perhaps even less! A class is just a class, not a stigma, not evidence of parental neglect, and certainly not a lifetime commitment to a new way of life.

• **Shop around.** If you're interested in exploring your Jewish "half," visit several synagogues and *havurot* (small, informal Jewish worship-and-social groups). Ask about their membership requirements, educational and social opportunities, and fee structure. Talk to other members. Quiz the rabbi on whatever subject is dearest to the Jewish side of your heart—the Palestinian situation, *Pirke Avot* (a section of the Talmud dealing with ethical standards), patrilineality, or where to find the best pastrami.

We've never seen a *shul* make a special effort to court the adult descendants of intermarriage, but many Reform, Reconstructionist, and Conservative synagogues are becoming much more sensitive to the needs of interfaith couples and their children. While our concerns are *not* precisely the same as theirs, a synagogue's or *havurah's* attitude toward such families is a pretty good indicator of how warmly they'll receive the descendants of intermarriage who aren't kids anymore.

• **If you're a secular, atheist, or agnostic Jew, look for a humanist *havurah*, synagogue, or organization.** You will then be able to participate in Jewish life-cycle rituals without compromising your convictions.

• **If you're a Jewish-identified descendant of intermarriage, take pride in the strength of your commitment.** If you're feeling a bit insecure and lonely within the Jewish community, remember that the Jewish-identified descendants of intermarriage will comprise the majority of American Jews within four decades. As our presence grows, our collective discomfort in Jewish surroundings will ease.

• **If you're a Christian, seek out a church, worship group, or humanist gathering that is unperturbed by your status as a descendant of intermarriage.** Steer clear of churches that insist that your non-Christian relatives are going straight to hell if you don't act fast to get them to convert. That's not your responsibility. Realize that your beliefs are your own, and that your interfaith family, already exquisitely sensitive to matters of creed and identity, will turn off quickly if pressured.

• **At church and elsewhere in the Christian community, take pleasure in your knowledge of your two worlds.** From it, you gain a rare, "hands-on" appreciation of Christianity's Jewish roots. If Jewish friends or relatives try to shame you for your adherence to Christ, remind them that in a free society, anyone may choose his or her own religion. Take advantage of your unique insights to encourage Christian understanding of the Jewish world and to discourage anti-Semitism.

• **Be wary of Christian churches and congregations that claim a special mission to "save Jews."** No matter how benevolent a particular Messianic Jewish organization sounds, or how appreciative they seem of your "Hebrew Christian" background, or how many Jewish trappings they display (listed under "Synagogues" in a Maryland telephone directory, for example, is a "Messianic Jewish Synagogue celebrating Torah and Israel's Messiah Yeshua [Jesus]"), the fundamental goal of these groups is the total absorption of world Jewry by Christianity. And while proponents of Messianic Judaism say that one can simultaneously be a Jew and a Christian, both Judaism and Christianity consider *anyone* who accepts Christ as his or her Savior or preeminent spiritual teacher or master to be a Christian.

• **Be honest about your choices with yourself and others.** Consider the implications that your spiritual and ethnic choices will have on your relationships with your family and

93

friends. Will choosing Judaism or Christianity make your life more joyous or more difficult? Do the pluses outweigh the minuses? Can you realistically expect support for your decision from the people you're closest to? (We *hope* so!)

• **You're not alone.** Wear your dual heritage proudly in your Jewish or Christian community, and look for historical role models. Today, the descendants of intermarriage have made their mark in every field of endeavor, and we've done so throughout history, although our dual heritage hasn't exactly been shouted from the rooftops. Few Christian-identified descendants of intermarriage, for example, are aware that Saint Teresa of Avila was the child of a Jewish man and a Christian woman.

• **No matter what spiritual and ethnic choices you make, expect some ongoing discomfort.** It's the nearly inevitable price of being permanently bonded to two worlds. Feeling this way doesn't mean you're emotionally disturbed, handling things badly, or have made the wrong choice. Vespers may still resound in the inner ear of a Jewish-identified descendant of intermarriage, while one who's chosen Christianity may wince at every critical reference to Jews in the New Testament. Feelings of duality are *normal* for us.

If you gave up some activity or ritual that you truly loved in order to assume a new religious or cultural identity, accept the pain. It may lessen in time, but there's no pill or potion that offers instant relief. Both Judaism and Christianity suggest that solace may be found in offering a continuing discomfort to God, and asking that it be used to increase one's spiritual growth.

• **Don't fret too much about fitting in ethnically in your chosen community.** Judaism stresses—and Christianity concurs—that God is interested in *avodah shebalayev* (the service of the heart), not in how you came to Him, or whether you physically resemble your fellow congregants. Hopefully, those around you will follow God's lead. (An Orthodox Jew once told us jauntily that at his synagogue, "We don't *care* if you're a *ger* [convert], as long as you're *there*.")

• **No matter how you choose to affiliate, don't denigrate the choices made by others in your interfaith family.** It is a sign of maturity and diplomacy to respect—without editorializing—the decisions of relatives who have opted for different paths. "I always wrap December presents in one of two kinds of paper, depending on the recipient," advises Donna, a Christian-identified adult child of intermarriage who is the mother of three grown children, two of whom are Jewish.

Two kinds of paper. That pretty much sums up the descendants of intermarriage. We all have two kinds of "wrapping paper" in our closets. We may scarcely touch one variety from year to year, while the other is replenished regularly. But we can learn to appreciate both, and the many nuances that comprise our spiritual and ethnic identities. Once we've achieved that, we have learned to celebrate our innate diversity, rather than fighting it.

CHAPTER

5

Homes of Our Own—Our Relationships, Our Children

My wife's rabbi refused to perform a marriage ceremony unless I converted. I was devastated. It nearly drove me completely away from my heritage.
                                            —ARNIE, POLITICAL CONSULTANT

I accept my "two halves" position. . . . However, I'd like to meet another half-Jew who believes the way I do, and maybe have children who are happier and better off than we are.
                                            —NICHOLAS, WELFARE WORKER

ROBIN HEARD THE TELEPHONE PERSISTENTLY SUMMONING HER as she unlocked her apartment door one winter morning a couple of years ago. *Rrring, rrring.* "Who could be calling me at eight o'clock?" she asked herself. After a long night of proofreading at a busy law firm, Robin yearned for sleep, but she picked up the receiver anyway.

At the other end of the line was Catherine, a young professional woman Robin once had spoken with briefly. She exclaimed, "I'm so glad I caught you! Remember how I told you about the trouble I'm having finding men to date who have a background like mine? Do you think you could help me?"

Robin grunted noncommittally and tugged off her slushy running shoes. "Refresh my memory a little," she suggested to Catherine, who began:

96

I know this sounds weird. Let me explain. My father was a Jew, and my mother was Catholic. When they got married, they each kept their own religion, but they agreed to raise me as a Catholic, which they did, and everything seemed fine.

My mother died recently, and since then, it's like—does this happen with other children of intermarriage?—it's like my father has gone crazy. He's on my case constantly to marry a Jewish man and give him Jewish grandchildren!

I don't know what to do. It's *so* unfair. He agreed to raise me as a Catholic. And I have trouble whether I go out with Jewish *or* Christian guys. Either way, they just don't understand, always giving me grief about being "half and half." I keep thinking that if I got involved with a man who's also from a mixed marriage, things would be *so* much easier. Do you know anyone that you could fix me up with?

Robin drew a deep breath. "You must understand, finding a man who's in your situation *might* make for a smoother relationship, but it's not a sure thing," she stressed. "And people like us, in our twenties and thirties and forties, are just the tip of the iceberg. Interfaith couples are having babies right and left, but remember, the majority of the children of intermarriage alive today are, well, still jailbait."

"I see," Catherine replied glumly. "Even if you knew someone who was available, there's no guarantee that we'd hit it off just because we're both children of intermarriage."

"Precisely. I'm in the same boat. Most people in our age group end up with someone who has two Jewish or two Christian parents," said Robin.

As Catherine awkwardly ended the conversation, Robin felt profoundly angry with herself. Why had she snapped at Catherine, who was looking for empathy, not a lecture?

She certainly hadn't been the first descendant of intermarriage who'd asked her to play matchmaker. Searching her conscience, Robin had to admit that Catherine's questions had hit a nerve, since she herself often felt that most of her born-Jewish and born-Christian friends really didn't understand or accept her "two halves."

As we begin to form lasting adult relationships, we find that our concerns about identity are not shared by our contemporaries who come from same-faith homes. Whether we consider ourselves straight, bisexual, or gay, whether we marry early or play the field indefinitely, descendants of intermarriage tell us that it can be a real struggle to accommodate our religious and ethnic duality in relationships with friends, partners, or spouses who were raised by two Jewish or two Gentile parents.

A number of our questionnaire respondents report that at one time or another in their lives they have been seriously involved with another adult child of intermarriage. In general, they say that while their status was a nice thing to have in common, it wasn't enough to base a relationship on, as Catherine forlornly hoped. Yet, some descendants of intermarriage who've married people like themselves say that their shared status is a plus, as Jeff does. The son of a Jewish man and Christian woman, raised in "American white-bread suburban style," Jeff remarks that his wife's background is "definitely positive for us, as neither of us had to deal with the other parents' religious problems."

Writer Dorothy Parker and her second husband, Alan Campbell, also were reared by interfaith parents. "Alan, like Dorothy, was half a Scot and half a Jew. From earliest childhood he, like her, had been made to feel a stranger within the gates, and their shared feeling of anomaly lay at the base of what was in every way a complementary marriage," noted Parker biographer John Keats.

Although they divorced once and remarried, the two stayed together, still squabbling and drinking heavily, until Campbell's death. However troubled the Parker-Campbell marriage was at times, at its core lay a deep mutual understanding of the cultural and religious contexts from which Dorothy and Alan had emerged, which appears to have softened the vehement discomfort and distaste with which Parker viewed her half-Jewishness.

Of our respondents who are still perched on the fence regarding their primary religious and cultural allegiance, men as well as women say that their ultimate choice of partner will have a great influence over whether they will live a secular life, affiliate as a Jew or as a Christian, or will follow a third path.

A number of the single people we've asked agree with Jeanne, a Jewish-identified divorced woman in her late thirties, who notes, "I think my difficulty and ambivalence in finding a mate has something to do with my mixed background." Bachelor Jamal adds, "I thought I'd affiliate as a Jew when I was a child, because I went to a Reform Jewish religious school for nine years. As I have matured, my views have changed somewhat. Much will depend on who, if, and when I marry."

For those adult children of intermarriage who were raised in stable homes in which their mixed status was not a major issue, becoming involved with an individual from a different religious or ethnic group may cause them to confront for the first time the full array of implications presented by interfaith relationships. Raised as a "real" Jew, Nora reports that her mother, who had converted from Methodism to Judaism before her marriage, became alarmed when her daughter began dating a man of Irish Catholic descent. "I think she was disappointed that I hadn't held out for a Jewish man," Nora says, adding:

I protested, "But, Mom, you of all people should understand!"

"I know, I know," she said, "but your father will be so disappointed." I wonder if she feels she failed in her adopted identity as a Jewish wife and mother? And would I feel the same way if I had children, raised them as Jews, and were faced with the same situation?

In a sense, I *do* feel as though I'm betraying my faith, and sometimes I *do* wonder if I should look more actively for a Jewish partner. My boyfriend's family has welcomed me with open arms, but I still feel a little strange celebrating Christmas and Easter with them. I'm relieved when New Year's Eve comes around—at least it's nondenominational.

I found out recently that my boyfriend attends Mass more often than he'd admitted to me at first. It's started me thinking about joining a synagogue and coming to terms with what I believe in. . . . I will admit that I feel very much an outsider when my boyfriend's family talks about Catholic-school experiences. When I saw him make the sign of the cross while attending a wedding, I felt uncomfortable, almost hurt.

Nora articulately voices some of the concerns that become very real to the descendants of intermarriage when entering into a serious relationship. We may find that we must reexamine our parents' wishes while still accommodating our own.

Some big-hearted interfaith parents are relieved to see their undecided children make a choice—any choice—as Bernard did. When he married his wife, who had lost all four of her Jewish grandparents (including a born-Gentile maternal grandmother) in the Holocaust, Bernard's Roman Catholic mother sent the couple "beautiful *Shabbat* candle holders," he recalls fondly. "When I asked her why she had given them to us, she told me that she had been very upset when I had no religious affiliation, and she was happy to see me grounded again," says Bernard.

Just as marrying an American citizen provides an immigrant with instant status as a legal resident, descendants of intermarriage frequently concede that an endogamously raised partner or spouse may serve as our passport to a new world, *regardless* of our sexual orientation. Hiding behind one's partner demonstrates understandably low self-esteem on our part. However, being involved with or married to someone whose religious and ethnic status is unambiguous makes it harder for a community to slight a descendant of intermarriage who clearly wants to commit to that culture, and possibly to raise children as "real" Jews or "real" Christians—an option that has also been contemplated by our bisexual and gay respondents.

Conversely, a descendant of intermarriage who feels little pull to either of his or her "halves" may say, as Rose does, "My brother and I married Gentiles not just because my [Jewish] father did, but because—if there is a reason—we had no religious affiliation and therefore no good reasons not to." Like a number of other such descendants, Rose found that while her growing involvement in Jewish life eased her spiritual dilemmas, it caused problems on the home front. "By the time I became more religious, I was already deeply involved with the man who became my husband. In many ways, I regret marrying out, but it's way too late," she laments.

Like their interfaith parents before them, when descendants of intermarriage begin planning their weddings, a great many previously unresolved issues surge to the surface with all the force of a swimmer evading a shark: What am I? What kind of life do I want to lead? How will I raise my children? Although these huge, frightening matters are often put aside while the couple concentrates on other wedding details, they compound interest, so to speak, if they are not at least partially resolved before the ceremony.

Although none of our respondents reported trouble in finding Christian clergy to officiate at their weddings, the rabbis they approached appeared just as ambivalent or negative about presiding as they often are when contacted by a "real" Jew engaged to a non-Jew. Patrilineal descendants who have not yet converted to Judaism say almost unanimously that the rabbis they contacted considered them, in the words of one irritated groom-to-be, "no better than a Gentile," even if they were in the process of or contemplating conversion to Judaism, and even if they were engaged to Jews and promised to raise their children in the faith.

Descendants of intermarriage who were raised as "real" Jews encounter the same problems with the rabbinate as "born" Jews who are planning to marry Gentiles, as Lindsey relates,

> It was a horrible problem getting someone to marry us, and I still resent the hoops we had to jump through and the abuse we took. It seems if we wanted a Jewish ceremony, that means that we're committed to making a Jewish home, and my husband shouldn't have been made to feel like the enemy—and me as a traitor—when we are adding Jews, not subtracting them.

Now the mother of two, Lindsey says that she still hasn't joined a synagogue. "It's a difficult choice," she says. "My husband is very interested in Judaism, although he doesn't want to formally convert. Perhaps when our daughters are older we'll join a liberal Conservative synagogue, if there is such a thing. I'd like them to go to [a synagogue] Sunday school, and we are raising them Jewish."

Our partners and spouses. In addition to our natural at-

traction toward a prospective partner, descendants of intermarriage often hope—consciously or not—that our unions
with "born" Jews or "born" Christians will ensure that our
homes will embody many of the rituals of Jewish or Christian
culture.

Maybe. Or maybe not, as Roberta, the daughter of a Jewish
man and Gentile woman, discovered. "Our wedding was
the only religious activity that my Jewish husband has ever
participated in," she remarks. Roberta's husband remains
steadfastly opposed to observing religious holidays and to
enrolling their two young daughters in a synagogue Sunday
school, explaining, "Whenever I say something about Judaism or about maybe the children having a Jewish education, he says, 'That's ridiculous! You're not even Jewish!' "

As our born-Jewish or born-Gentile spouses grow and
change, they may pressure us in a fashion that emphasizes
the split we feel between our "two halves." Nancy, who for
more than a decade was by far the more devout partner in
her marriage, felt this tension keenly as her secular Jewish
husband gradually became much more observant. Daughter
of a Jewish man and a Protestant woman, Nancy had been
a practicing Catholic since high school. She says:

> Early in our courtship and marriage, the religious difference
> between my husband and myself did not bother me at all.
> Indeed, I was excited about the possibility of creating a
> truly interfaith family, in which Christianity and Judaism
> could be equally affirmed and accepted. From a psycho-
> logical standpoint, I think that I was trying to heal my
> inner sense of being "split" by letting my husband take
> care of the Jewish part of me. I looked forward to claiming
> that part of myself through him.

However, after the births of their children, Nancy was
surprised when, as she recalls:

. . . my husband made it clear that our children would have a Jewish education or no religious education at all. The idea that Christianity would somehow hurt our children struck me as especially painful and almost incomprehensible. I was miserable, but it wasn't over yet. It seemed that my continued attendance at Mass, even by myself, bothered and threatened my husband, who was now obsessed with the need to ensure that our children would identify as Jews. He feared that I would be a bad influence on them!

Several years ago, Nancy relates, "after much soul-searching, psychotherapy, and spiritual direction from a Catholic laywoman, a kind of substitute mother who, unlike my own mother, essentially told me to go in peace," she converted to Judaism. "My conversion was a kind of negative leap of faith, made in spiritual darkness," she says, "but it seemed like the right thing to do."

She has since become more comfortable in the Jewish community, but Nancy's grief at being forced to put aside one of her "halves" is familiar to many descendants of intermarriage. They find it particularly painful to have to saw off one "half" in a home of one's own, after prolonged spiritual seeking. The experience of Nancy and others in her situation proves once again that nothing is static, even religious identity.

Like other descendants of intermarriage, Nancy also must deal with her parents' expectations about how she and her children will identify. Although her father has practiced no religion since leaving his Orthodox Jewish home as a young man, Nancy remarks, "He's really pleased that I'm raising the kids as Jews. But my mother is very unhappy about it." In fact, Nancy's mother seldom misses an opportunity to air her grievances. "The last time I took the kids to visit my parents, my daughter asked Mom, 'Why doesn't Uncle Ted get married?' Right away, she answered, 'I certainly wish he would, so I'll have some grandchildren to celebrate Christmas with,' " says Nancy.

Descendants of intermarriage tell us that even if we live secular or Christian lives, we may be considered Jewish by our in-laws. Such stereotyping can take a benign form, as Andrew, a thrice-married journalist, relates. The son of a Jewish man and a Gentile woman raised in a fundamentalist Christian home, Andrew is religiously unaffiliated. "The most difficult experience in my whole life has been my confrontation with my belief in God and my need to find a way to express it," he says. Although Andrew is strongly drawn by the Catholic Church, his present wife's father doesn't perceive him as a fellow Christian, and said to him, "I'm glad Rebecca married a Jew because I know you'll take good care of her."

Stereotyping also can hurt, as Mary Sue attests. The daughter of a Jewish man and Episcopalian woman, she mentions repeatedly that she and her Gentile husband were married in a Unitarian church "because no one else would have us." Although not Jewish-identified, she says she's perceived as such anyway, noting bitterly, "My husband and his family treat me like a stinking Jew and told me I should handle all the household finances because Jews 'are so good with money.' "

As we'll explore further in chapter 6, bearing the "stigma" of being Jewish even if one actually doesn't live as a Jew cuts deeply, even if experienced indirectly. One Episcopalian woman, raising three children from her failed marriage to a Jewish man, says that her mother recently rescinded her standing offer to give the oldest, Christian-identified girl a summer vacation abroad. Snorting with angry laughter, the divorcee recalls her mother's feeble excuse: "Mama said, 'Your daughter's last name is Jewish, and Europeans don't like those people.' "

Different lifestyle, same issues. The gay, bisexual, and lesbian descendants of intermarriage we surveyed don't differ noticeably from their heterosexual counterparts when it comes to how they feel about their dual heritages. The difficulties that these individuals face in finding a secure niche in a predominantly heterosexual society are well known, but being gay or bisexual enhances these respondents' feelings of "otherness" and complicates their efforts to find a spiritual and ethnic home.

Zoe, the daughter of a Jewish woman and a Methodist man who later converted to Judaism, is very much aware of her duality. She says:

> I never feel like I'm a "real" Jew—I'm gay, I don't act stereotypically Jewish, and I don't feel comfortable around Jews. I expect a sense of sharing, bonding, and togetherness that never exists.
>
> I'm uncomfortable with Conservative and Reform synagogues—I'd never go to an Orthodox one—because of the implicit heterosexuality and the assumption that you have a middle-class income. I feel invisible there.
>
> My daughters will be raised Jewish, but I plan to adopt them—internationally is the only possible way for lesbian couples. It will be harder for them not to be white European Jews.

Despite her unease in some Jewish surroundings, Zoe lights *Shabbat* candles, celebrates Jewish holidays, and attends a gay synagogue monthly.

Some of our respondents note with dismay that sharing a lesbian, gay, or bisexual orientation with one's fellow members of a gay church or synagogue doesn't necessarily mean that these "real" Christians or "real" Jews will understand a dual religious and cultural identity. Although one might presume that such institutions offer a more comfortable ambiance than a congregation composed primarily of "straight" families, some gay, bisexual, or lesbian descendants of intermarriage report that they still feel conspicuously "different," as Conor did. A grandchild of intermarriage, with his Irish father's surname and fair coloring, Conor recalls:

> I was raised as an Episcopalian, and at the age of fifteen I decided to live as a Jew. I also came out then, and was very proud of being gay and being a Jew. I studied Hebrew when I was in high school. Later I joined a gay synagogue, and the experience was awful. Every time they called me to the Torah, they'd say, "Here comes our Irish mick!"

Disgusted, Conor left, intending to become a member of a conventional Reform synagogue. Yet he found that his proficiency at *davening* (reading aloud from the Hebrew sections of the prayer book) made him conspicuous even there:

> I just wanted to be accepted as a Jew and *pray*, all right? And at my first service, the old lady next to me said, "Young man, you must be a convert. You certainly don't *look* Jewish, and you *daven* so beautifully—only converts *daven* that well!"

While bisexual and gay descendants of intermarriage, like their heterosexual counterparts, also may see their born-Jewish or born-Gentile partners as passports into their chosen religious and ethnic community, here too the dynamics are tricky. It is difficult to find clergy who will officiate at a same-sex holy union within a mainstream denomination, and even if such a ceremony is performed, these couples don't enjoy the legal and social legitimacy of heterosexual spouses in the Jewish and Christian communities. As our respondents have vouched, bisexual and gay descendants of intermarriage can and do establish happy homes and find their places in their chosen communities, but they face even more obstacles to nest-building than do their heterosexual counterparts.

Our children as children. When we descendants of inter-marriage have children of our own, we may end up handing off our unresolved identity dilemmas, like the baton in a relay race, to the next generation. As every parent knows, the birth of children forces us to confront issues that have not been dealt with actively since our childhoods—if ever. If our child is born at a particularly turbulent time in our lives, it may bring long-dormant family disputes abruptly to the surface, as it did for Cynthia. She remarks that her out-of-wedlock pregnancy at age eighteen served to step up "the warfare between my parents, which was exacerbated by their widely varying backgrounds, New York versus West Virginia."

Her mother, says Cynthia, raised her as a "socially conscious atheist, but she occasionally remembered that she was Jewish—she's very proud of being a *kohen* [a Jew who has priestly status]." Although she had given her own two daughters first and middle names that are not common among Jewish women, Cynthia's mother suddenly became urgently aware of her Jewishness right after her granddaughter was born. Says Cynthia:

> In all innocence, I had chosen the name Elizabeth Marie. When my mother saw the birth certificate, she asked, "What'd you name her *Mary* for?"
> Still weak from giving birth, I said, "It isn't Mary."
> Mom snapped, "It's a *form* of Mary."
> "Mara is a Hebrew name," I said.
> "The *Hebrew* form of Mary is *Miriam*," Mom persisted.
> I finally got her to drop the subject by getting an outspoken friend to tell her that she was being an idiot.
> I feel a situation like this results when a parent expects

a child to absorb a religious identity through osmosis. It seems unlikely to me that this exact scenario would happen in an unmixed household.

The naming is only the beginning. Although Cynthia considers herself and her daughter, now in her early twenties, to be halachically Jewish, Elizabeth is now a "fairly fervent Protestant, partly by default," Cynthia notes. "My attempt to introduce her to Jewish culture was stymied partly by her stepfather—my ex-husband—and partly by a lack of cooperation from the local [Jewish] congregation."

Even when descendants of intermarriage have assumed a primary religious identity in which they are striving to raise their children, they may step hesitantly. Institutional uneasiness with their mixed heritage plays one part. And if we were raised as "nothing," or if we affiliate with a religious culture that is different from the one in which we came to maturity, we may feel faintly fraudulent as we tailor religious ritual to our children's needs. Betty, the biological daughter of a Gentile woman and a Jewish man, who was raised by secular Jewish adoptive parents, remarks:

> My husband is from El Salvador. He's a Catholic by upbringing, and now by choice. I myself have been a practicing Catholic and Christian for about ten years now. Our three children are Christians, but I find it hard to transmit child-appropriate church "doctrine," as I wasn't myself a Christian child.

Secular descendants of intermarriage who lack a strong commitment to either of their "halves" often allow their spouses to call the tune in giving their children a primary religious identity, even if this makes them feel somewhat uncomfortable. "I feel no *religious* affiliation," says Michael, a physician in his forties. "I value both my urban-Jewish-intellectual and hillbilly-coalminer-farmer heritages, yet *culturally* I think of myself as a Jew." When asked how he feels that interfaith couples should raise their children so that they can most successfully come to terms with their dual heritages, Michael admits, "I sure don't know," adding:

> My wife takes our kids to the Catholic church and CCD [Confraternity of Christian Doctrine] classes, but they attend public school. We try to teach them some about Jewish religion and culture. I secretly hope they'll reject this Catholic stuff when they grow up.

What about Christmas? Our respondents who are raising, or contemplating bearing, children of their own find that Christmas remains a powerful, potentially divisive, emotionally loaded symbol for them, just as it was for their interfaith parents. While downplaying its significance as a religious holiday, some Jewish-identified descendants of intermarriage who celebrated Christmas as they were growing up find that it may be the last vestige of their quasi-Christian childhoods that remains in their adult lives.

Like their interfaith parents before them, Jewish-identified descendants of intermarriage who enjoyed celebrating Christmas as kids often wonder how—or if—they should pass along the holiday's secular pleasures, along with their own childhood memories. Will celebrating a secular Christmas totally confuse their own children, or compromise their budding Jewish identity?

Even those descendants who grew up in strongly Jewish milieus wonder how to observe Christmas in some fashion that doesn't threaten their children's nascent Jewish identity, as Valerie hopes to. The daughter of a Jewish man and a Gentile woman, Valerie was raised in a "totally Jewish" environment. Today, she considers herself "nontheistic" and rejects the idea of formal conversion to Judaism, as "I've never felt comfortable in Jewish synagogues and other groups." Now married, Valerie notes:

> Remarkably, my Mexican-American mother-in-law requested that we raise our daughter as a Jew, and so she will attend Jewish Sunday school. My husband and I will observe the Jewish holidays and traditions, but we will also have a Christmas tree—although that's about it as far as Christian traditions are concerned.
>
> Kids have to feel good about their whole selves, including diverse heritages. I celebrated both traditions as a child, and will do the same for my child.

Some Jews might say that Valerie's daughter, with just one Jewish grandparent—and the "wrong" one, at that—isn't really Jewish. However, Valerie's efforts to plant the seeds of Jewish identity in her daughter, while respecting her own Christian "half's" longing for Christmas, as well as her husband's Christian identity, illustrate how having families of our own may multiply our internal conflicts.

In an effort to honor her interfaith parents' efforts to teach her about both her "halves," Shira plans to do the same with her offspring. The daughter of a Jewish man and an atheist, Methodist-raised woman, Shira says she received an "agnostic and eclectic upbringing, exposed to both Jewish and Christian customs and beliefs." She converted to Judaism as an adult and married another patrilineal descendant of intermarriage; the couple is now saving to buy a home, join a synagogue, and start a family of their own.

"We plan to raise our child or children as Reform Jews, but my husband and I will expose them to the Christian customs we experienced as children. Specifically, we'll celebrate Christmas, but minus church and the carols. I do worry about negative responses to our celebrating Christmas when we do join a synagogue," Shira muses. She says that she feels the presence of her "two halves" most strongly at Christmastime. "I like the magic," she says, "but I suspect many full-blooded Jews feel this way, too."

Many of the lessons that descendants of intermarriage have learned—both positive and negative—from watching our interfaith parents in action can be used to good effect as we mature and establish relationships and homes of our own. Here is our housewarming gift to you, which we hope will be more useful than another set of monogrammed cerise towels, or even an espresso pot:

• **Don't let a friend, partner, spouse, or in-law put you on the defensive about your "two halves."** Ambivalence about our murky religious and ethnic status may prompt unpleasant remarks from the people to whom we are drawing closer. Explain what you can, turn the other cheek when you must. Provide an avenue for discussion by giving concrete examples of how a particular situation makes you feel. One woman whose mixed descent made her born-Jewish husband edgy reports that a fruitful discussion ensued when she remarked to him, "You know, I don't want to celebrate Christmas anymore, but I *loved* it when I was a child. It seems that you become tense if I reminisce about the heaps of presents under the tree, and the way that my family would go caroling from house to house in our neighborhood. Do you feel that my memories are incompatible with living as a Jew now?"

When your partner or spouse begins to spar with you about whether you're "really Christian," or "Jewish enough," he or she may feel that coming from an endogamous home—even one that was totally secular—suffices to give him or her the upper hand in any argument about religious or ethnic legitimacy. We've found that such sparring is as common to gay and bisexual relationships as it is among heterosexuals. And however wrong-headed they may appear, these attitudes will not change quickly.

Only you can decide if your partner's or spouse's distrust of your background is profound enough to damage or destroy the relationship. Stay calm. Seek counseling if you feel the situation warrants it. Humor helps, too. One son of a born-Jewish-turned-Unitarian man and a Gentile woman decided to laugh rather than brood when his Jewish fiancée's father remarked, "Well, half a loaf is better than none!"

• **If you are of mixed Jewish-Gentile descent and plan to have children, remember that you need not live as a Jew in order to carry genetic disorders that are most commonly found among "born" Jews.** The best-known of these tragic maladies, Tay-Sachs disease, causes an apparently healthy baby to lose control of its newfound physical and mental abilities, starting at about six months of age. Gradually becoming blind, paralyzed, and unaware of its environment, a Tay-Sachs–afflicted child will inevitably die of the disorder, usually by the age of three or four years.

According to the March of Dimes, nearly one in twenty-five American Jews, primarily those of Central and Eastern European descent, carries a Tay-Sachs gene, although the gene may be transmitted by members of *any* ethnic group. If both parents are carriers, there is a one-in-four chance with each pregnancy that the child will inherit a Tay-Sachs gene from each parent and develop the disease. If only one parent is a carrier, none of the couple's children will develop Tay-Sachs, but each child has a fifty-fifty chance of inheriting the gene and becoming a carrier.

Even if your spouse has no known Jewish ancestors, if you are an adult child or grandchild of intermarriage, *both* you and your partner should undergo a blood test—preferably before conception takes place—in order to determine whether either of you carries the Tay-Sachs gene. Call your local hospital for a referral to a genetics clinic or center that performs Tay-Sachs testing.

• **Don't be afraid to start at the beginning, and learn a new**

religion or way of life right along with your partner or child.
Descendants of intermarriage, especially those who have
switched religious allegiances or were raised as "nothing,"
may frantically play catch-up as adults. The pressure is dou-
bled if they are trying to teach unfamiliar religious and ethnic
rituals not only to themselves but to their kids. Relax. Learn
at your own pace, and if you have children, learn as they
learn. There are a number of excellent resources, including
parenting guides, available to Jewish and Christian adults
who are new to a particular culture.

• **Try not to compare your home life or your parenting
style with that of friends who were raised by two born-
Jewish or born-Gentile parents.** Since we all want to create
an optimal home environment, insecure descendants of intermarriage are susceptible to yet another "solution fantasy":
that we would *automatically* know more, or know better,
about how to create a Jewish or Christian home, or how to
nurture a Jewish or a Christian child, if we had been raised
by parents of the same faith. Descendants of intermarriage
sometimes forget that our friends from endogamous homes
may be even less knowledgeable than we are about our
chosen ethnic and spiritual home bases.

This was rather forcefully demonstrated to Leslie at a coffee
party for the parents of new students at her elder son's
Conservative Jewish nursery school. The director explained,
"The children will be celebrating *all* of the Jewish holidays,
including some that you may not even have heard of. And
they'll be learning *brachot,* the blessings for food, for wine,
for *Shabbat* candles. . . ." As some of the parents began to
look alarmed, the director hastily reassured them, "Really,
they're easy—you'll learn them too!"

• **If you lead a secular life, please teach your child something about both of your birth cultures.** When a Christian
woman told us that her intermarried siblings were raising

their children as "nothing," she inquired, "What difference does it make if they lose their Jewishness?" We replied, as we have to many others who've recounted similar situations, that it's a sad thing to see *any* ethnic culture, whether Jewish or Christian, lost from a family because its members don't care enough to pass along to the next generation at least some small aspect in story, song, or ritual.

Secular descendants of intermarriage who are atheist, agnostic, or alienated from either or both of their religious "halves" often throw out the baby with the bathwater by openly denigrating their ethnic backgrounds as well. Not only does this send an ugly anti-Semitic or anti-Christian message to their children, but completely discarding one or both cultures may leave their kids with a spiritual and ethnic vacuum that they may later choose to fill in undesirable ways.

Secular descendants of intermarriage need not, however, fake a religious faith that they don't believe in, even "for the children's sake." Descendants of intermarriage who do not take comfort in religion per se will not compromise their beliefs by passing along family stories, cooking a remembered dish, enrolling a child in secular Jewish or Christian history courses or social groups, becoming involved with a political organization, a humanistic Jewish synagogue, or a Christian equivalent, or by exploring their geographic and genealogical roots. Ignoring your background serves no one—not you, and certainly not your children.

• **Descendants of intermarriage can—and should—draw from their mixed backgrounds in order to teach our children by our own example how to get along in a pluralistic world.** "I feel strongly that my duality has allowed me to accept ambiguity in life. I can accept diversity and lack of consensus when I realize others cannot," remarks Valerie. Such unique insights can help us remain nonjudgmental in potentially

volatile situations, especially within our interfaith families—
a priceless skill, for what can be more explosive than questions of faith and ethnicity?

• **Acknowledge that your extended family almost certainly
will be polyglot in its practices and beliefs.** As we saw in
the preceding chapter, our interfaith families may have a
hard time adjusting to the fashion in which we live out our
chosen spiritual and ethnic identities, especially if we deviate
from the agendas that they have prepared for us. The
stresses multiply as we pair off and raise children who live
as we do, supporting and reinforcing us in our choices.
Through our own fledgling families, we may be following a
way of life that is glaringly different from the one in which
we came to maturity, or from the paths chosen by our sisters
and brothers.

Consequently, descendants of intermarriage must accept
the fact that they and their siblings are likely to create homes
that follow widely divergent spiritual and ethnic paths. From
a very early age, our children will ask questions about the
dissimilarities they perceive among their relatives. We can
answer them in simple and nonjudgmental language, saying,
for example, "That funny writing in your cousin Alon's
workbook is Hebrew. That's the language that Jews use for
prayer. We are Christians, but one of your grandfathers was
a Jew." Or, "Your cousins get Easter baskets because they
are Christians, and Aunt Paula sends them to Sunday school
at a Congregational church. We have a Jewish home."

• **Do not feel obliged to compromise deeply held beliefs
in order to placate others in your extended family.** If your
in-laws, siblings, or other relatives celebrate holidays that
are not part of your life, your own comfort will gauge how
much you and your children will become involved. Some
Jewish-identified descendants of intermarriage might feel no
conflict in allowing their very young children to participate
in a family member's Christmas-tree–trimming party, for ex-

ample, while others would break out in hives at the idea. Let your conscience be your guide.

If you honestly feel that you must abstain from a family gala, don't conceal from your children the truth about the source of the conflict, as some experts advise. Let the kids know briefly but honestly what Uncle Doug believes, why your family doesn't live as he does, and do your best to find noncontroversial times to get together. Fortunately, plenty of holidays have absolutely no specific religious or ethnic content, such as the Fourth of July, Mother's Day, Father's Day, Labor Day, Veteran's Day, and Thanksgiving. And then there are always birthdays, Memorial Day, Groundhog Day, and so on.

• **Manners matter.** It's not necessary to practice your sister-in-law's religion or even to understand her way of life in order to commemorate what is important to her. (And, of course, you can hope she extends the same courtesy to you.) If you're normally pretty casual about things like RSVPs, thank-you notes, or sending greeting cards, uphold the very highest standards in etiquette when a family member's life-cycle event—baptism, *bris*, baby naming, confirmation, *bar* or *bat mitzvah*, wedding, or funeral—rolls around. At holiday time, many Christian-identified descendants of intermarriage report that they gladly send appropriate greetings on Hanukkah, Passover, and Rosh Hashanah to their Jewish-identified siblings and other relatives, who are happy to reciprocate at Christmas and Easter.

• **Let the past be past.** If you are attempting to plant in your children religious and spiritual roots that are different from yours, don't make a special effort to pretend that you've always lived as a Christian, as a Jew, as whatever—*especially* if you grew up in a secular home and are trying to give your children a grounding that you may have always secretly longed for. Descendants of intermarriage who have unsatisfactory or downright negative memories of their childhoods frequently admit that they wish they could rewrite history just a little bit. Lying, of course, is not recommended, and it isn't even necessary. Remember that children live very much in the present, even if *we* can't. Your day-to-day example has far more influence on them than whether you did or didn't have to attend catechism classes back in the Dark Ages.

• **Respect the choices that are made by your growing or grown children.** We've already stated that by virtue of establishing an interfaith home, our parents have lost the ability—if indeed parents ever have such a power—to guarantee that we would adhere to a particular faith or ethnic identity as adults. The same holds true for us, although it can be heart-wrenching to see a child turn away from a way of life that we ourselves cherish and can never take for granted.

Rena, for one, warmly accepts the religious paths pursued by her grown daughters. The daughter of a Jewish woman and a Gentile man who raised her as "nothing," Rena has always lived as a Jew, even during her brief marriage to a man raised in a Catholic family. "One of my daughters is a member of a Conservative synagogue, while the other is very active in her Episcopal church, its choir, and its other organizations. I am satisfied that they are happy where they are," Rena remarks.

If we yearn for acceptance and approval from our parents, relatives, spouses, friends, and the members of our chosen religious and ethnic communities—which we *do*—in turn we must show tolerance toward the choices made by our siblings and our own children. We can only hope that they'll exhibit the sunny optimism, sense of place, and respect for individuality that all parents want for their children. We also can wish for a little something extra—that they'll show great pride in their status as descendants of Jewish-Gentile intermarriage.

CHAPTER

6

In the Workplace, in the Meetingplace, as Citizens of the World

I'm very good at bridging the gap between people, ideas, and feelings. This is partly due to my upbringing in an interfaith home, partly character, and partly study.
—MELISSA, ADMINISTRATIVE ASSISTANT

Children of mixed marriages need, if anything, more protection from anti-Semitism than Jews need. If another Holocaust came, I am sure the children of intermarriage would be among the first to be persecuted.
—JASON, STATISTICIAN

"THAT BABY BROTHER OF YOURS," SAID ROBIN'S FATHER. "IT seems like every week, Christopher's got a different business deal that *just can't miss,* he says. And he wants me to invest in all of them." He shook his head. "Why can't Chris get an after-school job delivering pizzas, like everyone else?"

"Aren't you proud of him, Dad?" Robin asked. "He's putting himself through the theological seminary, and that takes gumption, doesn't it?" A fragment of family history flashed through her mind. She recalled her maternal great-grandfather Levine, who'd run a dry-goods store. And like his maternal grandfather Margolis (later Miles), Christopher has inquisitive green eyes and a restless desire to succeed in a business of his own, certain that even if prosperity weren't just around the corner, it might be just a short stroll away.

"Oh, Daddy, don't you see?" she laughed. "Christopher's Jewish 'half' is going to help pay his way until he becomes a Christian minister!"

Her father sighed with resignation, conceding, "You know, you might be right at that. I kept wondering where that kid was getting all of these wild business ideas. People in *my* family, we're bankers, we're solid, we're *conservative*. We tend to play it safe."

Like many other interfaith family members, Robin and her father find that when it comes to our choice of career, we are likely to be more amused than troubled by our efforts to balance our two "halves." For Christopher and many other descendants of intermarriage, how we earn our daily bread is likely to represent at least *one* demilitarized zone in the sometimes stormy relationships between interfaith parents and their children. While our questionnaire respondents spoke of many ways in which their mixed status has caused them dislocation or outright grief, relief and affection tended to pervade their stories of how their two cultures have affected their livelihoods.

When we asked Henry, a dentist, what influence his interfaith parents' birth cultures had upon his career path, he chortled, "Mama wanted a doctor!" His mother was Jewish. Christian mothers, of course, are just as pleased to see their offspring become professionally successful. But Henry's mother's outspoken wish typifies how our intermarried parents influence our professional goals in an endearingly benign form, rather than trapping a child between two often-contradictory sets of expectations.

When it comes to educational and professional goals, the descendants of intermarriage appear to be, for once, in the same boat with their endogamously raised peers. Since the majority of our questionnaire respondents are between the ages of twenty-five and sixty, they or their parents survived the Great Depression with renewed confidence in the merits of hard work and a good education. Kris, a nurse in her late forties, remarks:

Wanting to equal my [Protestant] father's educational ac-complishment is one of the factors that keeps me in this Ph.D. program when the going gets rough. I sometimes imagine that he can see and hear what I am doing, and I say, "See, at least one of your daughters is going to do what you expected us to do." He once threw a fit in a restaurant when he was told that my sister had flunked out of her first attempt at college. He had a big emotional investment in it.

The pressure to excel comes from both sides of the fam-ily. My Jewish grandfather refused to recognize the mar-riage of my parents until ten years after the fact. The idea slid down his gullet a little more easily when my mother showed him my father's diplomas.

The near-universal desire of parents to see their children flourish, even if it means surpassing them in achievement, appears to transcend cultural and religious differences. When describing our parents' and extended families' influence on our careers, descendants of intermarriage do so with a mea-sure of detachment, in a manner that goes far beyond pat ethnic stereotyping. "I grew up neither Jew nor Gentile yet temperamentally, genealogically both," says Diane P. Freed-man, a college English professor who was raised in neither tradition. She adds:

I have felt a mild but lingering guilt about not identifying equally with my parents' different heritages. But I have also found strength in resisting what may be the coercive aspects of each heritage: I always caricatured my relatives on my [Catholic] mother's side as people who said "be good" and those on my [Jewish] father's side as those who said "do well."

I suppose I feel I've done mostly the latter by becoming a poet-scholar, following in the tradition of my Jewish great-great-grandfather, who published books of Jewish philosophy and history in which four different speakers argue in poetry throughout. . . . In America, my Jewish relatives are all great students, if not writers; my own father recited Blake and Keats to me when as a child I watched him shave.

In contrast, most of my Catholic relatives today work blue-collar jobs. My maternal grandmother, wonderful gardener, seamstress, cook, never learned to read either Ukrainian or English; my grandfather the coalminer wasn't much of a reader or writer, though my mother tells me he was extremely gentle, a pacifist. But the enduring details of their life held me too.

I learned from them the pleasures of personal history and continuity in the face of my perceived conflicts and discontinuities. I grew proud of both of my heritages, envious of *Baba*'s enduring faith, her girlhood in the Ukrainian countryside, and her house in the Pennsylvania hills (Long Island is flat, our house on a dull, suburban grid), if more comfortable with my Jewish intellectual tradition and the reading and writing it has led me to do.

Not only do knowledge and understanding of our "two worlds" give us flexibility and tolerance, but descendants of intermarriage can and do put these qualities to work at our jobs, to our benefit. "I consider my between-two-worlds status helpful for me as a therapist," says Jeanne, daughter of a Jewish man and a "lapsed Catholic" woman. "I can feel empathy for outsiders, and being 'outside' myself helps me to observe what might be missed by others who are 'inside.'"

Another patrilineal descendant of intermarriage, Susan, says that her "perpetual outsider" status has made her a better journalist. "I can always see the world through someone else's eyes," she notes. And our acceptance of diversity as the status quo may even make it easier for us to get along with our co-workers. Bradley, an advertising executive, says, "I was brought up as both Presbyterian and Jewish. I went to a Catholic university and then worked for a Baptist film organization. I enjoyed working with them all, and also forgave them for *their* sometimes narrow and prejudiced views. I think they appreciated my objectivity."

As we mature, our dual status can enhance our careers. But growing up as an "outsider" who belongs to two worlds, but is not wholly part of either, can have a negative impact on our ability as adults to enjoy and nurture causes and groups. The great majority of our respondents, most of whom identify as Democrats, say that they are not politically active, join or contribute money to few or no political groups, and tend not to be "joiners" of other secular groups as well. A number of our respondents directly attribute their propensity to walk alone to their betwixt-and-between status as descendants of intermarriage.

As we've seen in previous chapters, our links to two worlds may make it very difficult to risk upsetting our interfaith parents by opting to settle in one religion or one culture. Evidently, our duality also makes it hard for us to assert strong beliefs by joining other groups as well. We have trouble tapping in to something larger than ourselves if we cannot determine just where, in fact, we belong.

Many of us saw our interfaith parents rejected by their families, communities, and congregations. As we'll see in the following chapter, when our parents lose or cut back our roots, we are likely to be deprived of much-needed adult role models in both the Jewish and Christian communities. Wariness, detachment, and objectivity are useful career traits, but they can and do hamper us from seeking out groups for socializing, worshipping, or sharing political goals.

Permanent duality. Regardless of how—or *if*—we affiliate, descendants of intermarriage say that it is not possible to turn our backs on the implications of a dual heritage. Even if we never seriously consider living a Jewish life, it is likely that we may suffer some anti-Semitic remarks or other negative fallout from our Jewish heritage, without the mitigating support and friendship of the Jewish community. A good many of the Christian-identified and secular descendants of intermarriage we've queried feel their "Jewishness" strongly—more powerfully, we suspect, than do some secular Jews who have two Jewish parents, for whom status and identity are likely to be a less emotionally loaded issue. Whether our feelings about our Jewish heritage are positive or negative is affected dramatically by the opinions of our families, friends, and the Jewish and Christian communities:

- "In good proto-Nazi fashion, most Americans have identified me not as half-Jewish and half-German but as all Yid. I bet most of your respondents will tell you the same thing," challenges the atheist son of a Jewish man and a Bavarian Catholic woman.
- "Although I am only one-quarter Jewish, I look Jewish, and people will assume I am of the Jewish faith. This gives me a split personality. . . . The only problem I have is with anti-Semites who think I am Jewish, so I can identify with Jews who have the same problem. I think it's easier, though, if you are Jewish entirely rather than part-Jewish. When you are only partly something, you are between the devil and the deep blue sea," says a religiously unaffiliated man whose maternal grandmother was Jewish.
- "I wanted to be Protestant. It seemed easier. Still does.

124

I tell my Christian friends I associate with the Hebrew faith because my husband is Jewish. I tell my Jewish friends that I do not conform to their religion because the rabbi doesn't accept me as a Jew. I play the victim. If I had to do it all over again, I would raise my children as Christians. I would never tell anyone about my Jewish heritage. I'm proud of it, it's just that it presents too many problems," remarks the daughter of a Jewish man and a Reformed Lutheran-raised woman who converted to Judaism as an adult.

- "There is a significant difference for those half-Jews who have a Jewish surname and appearance. Ironically, although the name is from the father, that lineage does not define you as a Jew. Yet, you are more likely to be perceived as one by the rest of the world, which puts you in a double bind," says the daughter of a Christian woman and Jewish man, who identifies with no religion.

- "I am seen by non-Jews as a Jew and by some Jews as a non-Jew. Despite the thousands of years of tradition, I think that this issue will be resolved soon to welcome us into the Jewish fold. Women used to be second-class citizens in Jewish culture—now they are rabbis. So things do change for the better," predicts the daughter of a Jewish man and a woman who renounced her Catholic upbringing.

- "My dual heritage remains the whole question of who I am. If being Jewish means that you're not part of general society, being half-Jewish means that you're neither a part of general society, nor are you truly part of Jewish society. Whatever it is, you're not it," says the secular Jewish son of a Jewish man and a Gentile woman who converted to Judaism before her marriage.

It's easy to see how our reluctance to join groups, seeded by our parents' visible displacement as interfaith couples, and our own internalized duality, is multiplied by our contacts with our two worlds. We've found that our innate duality also influences our attitudes toward the Holocaust and the state of Israel.

The Holocaust. Few would argue that the Holocaust, which claimed the lives of millions of Jews, descendants of Jewish-Gentile intermarriage, and non-Jews as well, is one of the greatest tragedies of human history. Some observers might be surprised at how powerfully our questionnaire respondents, regardless of primary religious and ethnic allegiance, feel kinship with the Holocaust victims. Christian or Jew, secular nonbeliever or Buddhist, the descendants of intermarriage we've queried not only freely express horror and revulsion at this widespread loss of life and community, but have stated in no uncertain terms that if, God forbid, such a situation arose again, they would do whatever they could to save Jews and others from anti-Semitic oppression.

"As a teenager, I felt almost heroic to declare my Jewishness, against an oppressive government and the very fresh memory of the Holocaust. I felt it was the only decent thing to do," says Irina, daughter of a Jewish woman and Roman Catholic man, who grew up in Hungary. "Now I know it was the *only* thing to do. A drop of Jewish blood is enough to be killed, if people decide to kill Jews. I might as well be proud of it."

All of the adult children of intermarried Holocaust survivors we queried, including those who live Christian or secular lives, appear to have a strong, almost mystical connection with Judaism. Elinor, "an inactive Unitarian," recalls, "My [Protestant] father and [Jewish] mother met in Germany and fell in love instantly. However, due to Hitler they were soon unable to even *meet* in public. In a long, complicated process, with the help of some friends and also some luck," her parents fled Germany and were able to settle and marry in New York.

"My brothers and I were always extremely aware of the

Holocaust, and fully realized what would have happened to our mother if she hadn't left when she did. Although we were raised as Protestants, I think that we all felt very close to our Jewish heritage," says Elinor.

If a parent's life was threatened by the Holocaust, it may motivate us to actively affiliate as a Jew, a number of descendants of intermarriage told us. Meg notes:

The Holocaust has definitely affected my life, and has been a great factor in determining my religious choices. It is difficult to be simplistic about how I would feel if the Holocaust were to take place in America. Being a child of a survivor made my Jewish heritage naturally strong and my choice to become a Jew an easy one.

My father's behavior as a parent was inconsistent and unreasonable due to his experiences. For example, anger would occur when one of his children would hurt themselves, instead of nurturing and soothing, because of his intense fear of losing anyone he loved.

My father probably married a non-Jew because of his rebellion toward the religion for what he had to experience and maybe his paranoia of continuing to be a victim of bigotry and hatred. He does not affiliate with the Jewish religion as much as he did as a child for those reasons, and because the religious holidays bring back memories that become quite painful to him. However, his pride as a Jew has always remained intact. As he grows older, that pride strengthens. It's why he is proud of his children, three of whom have chosen to become Jews.

Stand up and be counted. In the face of another Holocaust targeting Jews—certainly, a hypothetical situation that we pray would never come about—the descendants of intermarriage would mobilize quickly and forcefully to defend the Jewish people. The great majority of those we interviewed, irrespective of their ultimate religious or ethnic allegiances, stated in no uncertain terms that if the Jewish people were ever threatened again on such a mass scale, they would do whatever they could to save them.

Those we asked formally and informally almost unanimously agree that even descendants of intermarriage who are Christian-identified or following some other non-Jewish spiritual path retain a strong sense of kinship with the Jewish people, and would be their willing allies in times of trouble. Surprisingly, the Jewish community's coolness to interfaith families apparently has not depleted the reservoir of love and goodwill that so many descendants of intermarriage maintain to replenish their attachment to their Jewish "half."

Israel: What's in it for us? Virtually all the descendants of intermarriage we contacted say they maintain at least some emotional connection to the state of Israel. Not only is its existence a point of pride for our Jewish parent, but our Christian parent's religious traditions have long cherished the sacredness of the biblical homeland, filled as it is with sites that are holy to Christianity, Islam, and Judaism.

Unlike the Holocaust, the state of Israel does not appear to compel the same automatic loyalty from the descendants of intermarriage—but, as it turns out, we're not the only ones who feel this way. Although "born" Jews under the age of thirty-five appear to demonstrate roughly the same levels of involvement in religious observance and communal activities as their parents and grandparents, these younger Jews are more critical of Israeli policies and less committed to the idea that Israel must be vigorously protected at all costs, according to a 1989 study by the American Jewish Committee. "Younger Jews are less likely to see Arabs and Palestinians as threatening Israel's survival, and they are also less likely to regard many or most members of particular groups of American Gentiles as anti-Semitic," says Steven

M. Cohen of the AJC's Institute on American Jewish-Israeli Relations.

Reflecting, perhaps, how our "two halves" make it easier to view both sides of ethnic and religious issues, descendants of intermarriage and "born" Jews under the age of thirty-five are more ambivalent than "born" Jews from our parents' and grandparents' generations about Israel's position on several current issues. While nearly all of our respondents warmly endorse the existence of Israel as a Jewish state, a number say they're quite uneasy with the way Israel has been handling its ongoing conflict with the Palestinians.

"My late husband always used to say that regarding the Palestinian situation, the Israelis learned a little too much from the Nazis. I definitely agree with him there," remarks Tessa. A Holocaust survivor in her seventies, she is the daughter of a Lutheran man and a woman who, Tessa says, "was three-quarters Jewish, and evidently that was enough for Hitler."

Not surprisingly, the descendants of intermarriage we surveyed—three-quarters of whom are patrilineal—tend strongly to disapprove of the Israeli law that grants automatic citizenship only to those with a born-Jewish birthmother or one who converted under Orthodox auspices. The lineage of the father is considered irrelevant. Just 3 percent of our respondents feel positive or very positive about this law. Seventy-five percent expressed negative or very negative sentiments, often summing up their dismay in a few succinct words, as did Justine: "Unless the Israelis have actually located Judaism on the X chromosome, this law makes no sense."

Many descendants of intermarriage say that the thoroughly entrenched concept of matrilineality as a litmus test for "Jewishness" enhances the tendency of Jews to pinpoint our allegiances quickly—sometimes without even asking us how we identify—which often leads to yes-I-am, no-you're-not shouting matches. Consequently, the Israelis' tenacious retention of the matrilineal rule upsets our respondents on more than one level. Says George, son of a Jewish man and a Catholic woman:

> As a person declared to be illegitimate by this policy, I am offended. We are dealing here with human beings, not the pedigrees of prize cattle. Since the only immediately apparent advantage of being a Jew is that people all over the world who have never met you will hate you passionately, I cannot understand the point of the argument. It was my understanding that Israel's original position was that anybody who sincerely declared himself to be a Jew was entitled to the label.

Of our respondents who expressed an opinion about matrilineal descent in this context, 22 percent were ambivalent or didn't care. "I have no interest in moving to Israel, so it doesn't affect *me*," was a typical comment. But what about those descendants of intermarriage who *do* care about their status in Israeli society? Shulamit speaks eloquently of her firsthand experience with a number of Israelis who view her as marginally Jewish at best. The daughter of a secular Jewish man and a "Unitarian, ex-Catholic" woman, Shulamit underwent a halachic conversion after moving to Israel. Although she finds her Orthodox Jewish life deeply satisfying on many levels, she still feels set apart from the "born" Jews with whom she associates. She explains:

> In Israel, patrilineal [adult children of intermarriage] are not usually pressured to convert; they are told in no uncertain terms that they are *not* Jewish. If they try to convert, they have an easier time than people with no Jewish background.

Nevertheless, most of the time, a Jewish father is not taken into account as a basis for Jewish identity. Matrilineals sometimes feel stigmatized. I know one woman who hides the fact that her father is not Jewish. When she did tell a few Israelis, they reacted with fascination, asking her, "How does it feel to have a non-Jewish father?", not fathoming that to this woman, her dad was just her dad, and not some alien life form!

I don't know what the rate of intermarriage is in Israel, but I imagine it is very low, as there is no civil marriage, so a non-Jew must convert to marry a Jew. Some go to Cyprus to marry out. Conversion is a lengthy and difficult process, especially if the rabbinical court suspects potential converts of doing it just to get married. The first question they asked me was, "Do you have a boyfriend?", ignoring the fact of my Jewish background. However, I feel they were easy on me *because* of my father.

All of the patrilineal [children of intermarriage] I know here are either in the process of conversion or have received Orthodox conversions, the only kind that's recognized. We generally keep quiet about our non-Jewish roots, as there often is, unfortunately, prejudice against converts. We are not seen as any different from converts with no Jewish roots whatsoever.

Of course, not everyone is prejudiced, and I have often been seen as particularly "righteous" for having converted. But one patrilineal that I know who converted, and who is *very* religious, got into a bad marriage. The groom's mother wouldn't speak to her at the marriage. Later, when her husband got mad at her, he would call her a "filthy *shiksa*," ignoring both her very sincere conversion and her Jewish father.

Patrilineal descendants of intermarriage may find comfort in the American Jewish Committee's 1989 finding that 86 percent of the American Jews it surveyed believed that Israel should strenuously resist efforts by Orthodox groups to recognize only those conversions performed by Orthodox rabbis. Of those polled, 60 percent said that if only Orthodox conversions were recognized, some of their close friends or relatives who consider themselves Jewish would not be recognized as such by the state of Israel.

Perhaps more than any other recent issue, the Orthodox efforts in 1988 to amend the Israeli "Who is a Jew?" law sensitized American Jews to the concerns of the adult children of intermarriage. The question of *our* potential legitimacy as Jews became very real to millions of Reform, Conservative, and secular American Jews for perhaps the first time when their own validity as Jews was challenged by a powerful minority.

Another consciousness-raising factor among the American Jewish community is the soaring intermarriage rate. When the Jewish legitimacy of one's own grandchildren is at stake, what's been lovingly called "grandmatrilineality" ("*My* grandchildren are Jewish no matter which parent is a 'born' Jew!") will not suffice to give the descendants of intermarriage a Jewish identity.

While the rest of the Jewish and Christian world slowly becomes aware of the concerns of the descendants of intermarriage—many of whom, after all, have been privately brooding about their dual status for much of their lives—here are a few reminders:

• **If you are hesitant to join any groups at all, ask yourself why.** Since so many of our interfaith parents were rejected by their families, communities, and congregations, we may have inherited their "who needs *them?*" attitude. If that suits you, fine. But if xenophobia is shutting us off from the company of others for whom we may yearn, we're robbing ourselves of friendship, fun, contacts, and perhaps the chance to mold the world a little more to our liking. By our presence, involvement, and influence, we can encourage Jewish and

Christian groups to welcome the descendants of intermarriage who follow us.

• **Don't deny, ignore, or hide from anti-Semitism or anti-Gentilism.** Regardless of whether it's directed at you personally or at Jews or Christians in general, it is our duty to object to bigoted attitudes and remarks. Even so, many descendants of intermarriage, unfortunately, say they find it necessary to play down or conceal a dual heritage, as does Clement, an Episcopalian-identified union organizer. "I aspire to be a politician on a national level, and sometimes feel it would be better to be quiet about my Jewish background because of general American anti-Semitism," he notes. It's a shame Clement feels that way, as a number of grown children of Jewish-Gentile intermarriage—including Senator Barry Goldwater of Arizona, Senator William Cohen of Maine, and former San Francisco mayor Dianne Feinstein—*have* been successful at the polls, with their mixed ancestry neither a secret nor a campaign issue.

• **Be wary of committing your time or money to Jewish or Christian groups that don't openly welcome the members of interfaith families.** Fortunately, a number of big-name, big-budget groups, such as B'nai B'rith Women, have acknowledged changing times and demographics. BBW has gone out of its way to encourage descendants of intermarriage, as well as Gentile women married to Jewish men, to join. Other groups have not. You may have to take it upon yourself to make your background, needs, and desires known to less-enlightened organizations.

• **When giving money to Jewish or Christian groups that engage in overseas activities, inquire closely as to how their funds are allocated.** Philanthropy takes many forms, and while some worthy organizations relieve pain, hunger, and misery abroad, others engage in activities that may run directly counter to your interests. Make sure you know exactly how your donation will be spent. A number of Orthodox

Jewish groups operating in Israel with the support of American dollars have actively lobbied to drive interfaith families out of Judaism. Christian groups may send missionaries abroad who are intent upon converting the whole world to Christianity, a prospect that troubles Jewish-identified descendants of intermarriage. Ask before you give.

• **Any discomfort you may experience in Jewish or Christian secular groups is real.** Whether it's occasional or constant, feeling a bit uneasy among "born" Jews or Christians is part and parcel of life as a descendant of intermarriage. They often don't know how to deal with us, either. As our numbers and visibility increase, they'll learn, *especially* if we join them and make our needs known!

CHAPTER
7

Stressed Interfaith Families—Coming to Terms with Physical and Psychological Separation from Relatives, Divorce, Blended Families, Adoption, and Interracial Marriage

My dad realized that my mom wanted Jewish kids, so he went along with it and converted [from Methodism] to Judaism in 1964, before they were married. Since they divorced, he's become a "commercial Christian." He sends us Christmas cards, and makes slightly cynical anti-Semitic comments. I've been telling him to send me Hanukkah cards.

—ZOE, DELIVERYPERSON

Not having a religious affiliation, nor even having been exposed to either Judaism or Christianity, but knowing I am half of each, has been one of the worst stumbling blocks in my life. It caused me embarrassment and fear as a child, and caused me to lie on many occasions. I don't feel part of anything. The intermarriage also caused both of my parents to become cut off from their families, so I lost contact with my extended family. I have been unhappy most of my life and I attribute it, at least partially, to being a child of intermarriage.

—NATALIE, EDITOR

IN HEBREW, MIRIAM MEANS "BITTER," AN UNFORTUNATELY apt name for one older woman who told us what being a patrilineal child of intermarriage has meant to her.

"Since my mother was a Gentile, my status—or, more

135

accurately, my lack of status—among my Jewish family has affected me my whole life," Miriam relates. "My father's family didn't invite us to weddings or funerals, even though they'd chartered thirty limousines to chauffeur their friends. When my uncle died, I found out from the newspaper, not from them. My Jewish relatives were just the worst. My parents and I were always at the bottom of their sugar list."

After what Miriam terms "a lifetime of bitterness" about her rejection, she maintains only a tenuous connection with her Jewish heritage. We've found that anger like Miriam's is common to those all-too-numerous descendants of Jewish-Gentile intermarriage who have suffered one of the losses that is most characteristic of stressed interfaith families: erosion of extended family ties and resources.

Children of interfaith families whose emotional stability is taxed by such complexities as physical and psychological distance from extended family, divorce, stepparenting, adoption, or interracial marriage merit special attention. If the members of an interfaith family—not to mention the Jewish and Christian communities—cannot acknowledge their needs, these special conditions may trouble the family greatly and exacerbate any other existing problems. In frustration and rage, the troubled interfaith family may come to exhibit one or more of the serious dysfunctions discussed in chapter 8.

An interfaith family is not, as some researchers believe, inherently dysfunctional, a misconception we'll discuss at greater length in the following chapter. However, interfaith families *are* subject to certain unique stresses. Interfaith couples very commonly endure the criticism of relatives who disapprove of their decision to wed. Extended family may put their negative thoughts into action by cutting the couple out of their lives altogether, or by providing few or no opportunities for the interfaith couple to celebrate Jewish or Christian holidays or life-cycle events with them. Such rejection often fosters a "who needs *them?*" attitude on the part of the intermarried parents, who then have a difficult time teaching their children anything positive about one or both of their "halves."

Separation from one of their birth cultures can make a lifelong impact on a descendant of intermarriage, as Lynn attests. "As a child I was not allowed by my mother to spend much time with my father's relatives," she says, adding:

> I don't know if that was directly caused by their Judaism or by their general "otherness"—they weren't like us. As an adult, since my mother's death, it is almost wholly my Jewish relatives who are now family for me.
>
> I regret that such a division had to exist, particularly when I was a child and might have benefited from additional role models, from seeing other ways of being in the world. And now most of my mother's relatives are dead, so there's little chance for blending. It's sad.

If the interfaith parents fall out of touch with their families because of their marriage, the children learn an ugly lesson: *Family ties are expendable.* They also grow up knowing that in their isolation, they are likely to be considered less important to their extended families than are their cousins who have two Jewish or two Christian parents.

When interfaith parents are rejected by one or both of their families, or voluntarily keep their distance from them, their roots are forcibly pulled up. No matter how necessary interfaith parents may feel it is to forgo relationships with their extended family, or however loving they themselves may be to their own children, we cannot begin to compensate our parents for this crushing loss. Maintaining relationships with the families of both parents is important for the children and grandchildren of *any* marriage, and doubly so when we draw from two cultures.

Grandparents, uncles, aunts, and cousins provide more than just occasional babysitting and treats, or perhaps someone to pull pranks with at the Thanksgiving table. They represent family history and continuity. From the extended family a child learns what his or her parents were like when they were younger. If the family goes through tough times, relatives can provide emotional and financial support to the parents, and they may offer temporary or permanent shelter to the children. Or they may not, as tough-talking Lucille remembers:

My mother was half-Jewish, since her mother was a Jew. She married my father, who was Polish Catholic. So I'm only one-fourth Jewish, though I'm considered Jewish under Jewish law. Eventually my mother cracked up and went to a mental institution, where she had visions of Jesus and became a Christian. My father disappeared when I was seven and my brother was three, so we were sent to my two Jewish great-uncles and their families.

My brother was able to adapt to them, but I couldn't. I was only seven years old, but already a wild, bounce-off-the-walls kid—you can imagine what my home life had been like. I couldn't seem to live up to my Jewish uncles' expectations, and they had very little patience with me. Okay, I wasn't an easy child to deal with, and I don't want to put them down, but their whole attitude was that I was an imposition and only one-fourth Jewish besides. They eventually put me in foster care.

I'd like to be a Jew, and I look Jewish, I know. . . . But you can see why I just can't.

Lucille attributes her uncles' failure to care for her at least in part to her mixed descent. Whether or not that's the case, she became permanently alienated from Judaism and her mother's Jewish family, toward whom she expresses sorrow, anger, and regret.

"Both the Jewish and Christian communities should be careful not to exacerbate the emotional problems that interfaith families may face," cautions patrilineal, Jewish-identified Nancy, who adds:

> In my own case, I have seen my mother's Christianity heighten and validate her sense of victimization at my "betrayal" of converting to Judaism. When I attended services with her recently, the minister spoke of the need to continue to "witness," even when one feels rejected or is not listened to. The minister compared this sense of rejection to the feelings of the crucified Jesus! Needless to say, this was hardly a healthy message for my mother to hear.
>
> On the Jewish side, the frequent analogy drawn between intermarriage and the Holocaust is similarly destructive. At various times in my life when I was still a Christian, this message implied to me that so far as the Jewish community was concerned, I might as well be dead.
>
> Every family has emotional problems, of course. But for the children of intermarriage, these can be complicated by the longstanding warfare between the extended families and the faith communities of the parents. The descendants of intermarriage have to cut off half of their cultural heritage in order to be accepted by either community, and that is difficult enough. But when you add that each community believes that God and Truth are on its side—and most *do* believe this, no matter how much some liberals may protest—you can see how painful this conflict can become!

The loss of extended family makes many descendants of intermarriage feel somehow incomplete, even in stable interfaith homes in which a parent loses touch with his or her extended family because of distance and financial hardship, as was the case with Eloise.

Living in New Mexico, says Eloise, a retired teacher in her late sixties, her father was "the only Jew in town, and he just couldn't afford to return to his native Louisiana." Although she never met most of her Jewish relatives, Eloise said that her father corresponded with his sisters, and she grew up hearing stories about her cousins.

"In 1984 my cousin in North Carolina sent me photos and articles, and I put together an album of family genealogy, complete with photos—fifty-five of them!" she says. Warmed by her obvious interest, her Jewish relatives invited Eloise and her husband and children to *bar mitzvahs* in Louisiana and Texas, and she later accompanied several members of her extended family on a trip to Paris. "After meeting my relatives, I felt 'whole' for the first time in my life!" Eloise recalls joyfully.

Divorce. Marital stability among Jewish-Gentile couples appears even more precarious than among the endogamously married, according to a number of researchers, most recently Barry Kosmin of the North American Jewish Data Bank. Kosmin estimates that 32 percent of interfaith couples divorce, compared with 17 percent of Jews married to other Jews.

When an interfaith couple splits up, in pain and regret the custodial parent may abruptly cut off the children's connection to one of their "halves." Sometimes the line goes dead permanently. "When my [Christian] first wife and I split up, she threw everything Jewish out of the house, including me and the rye bread," Neil mournfully told us. His former wife restricted his contact with their daughters, raising them as Christians; Neil and his present wife, who is Jewish, have no children. The fact that he probably will never have a Jewish grandchild grieves him terribly. "My two younger girls aren't interested in Judaism. The oldest married a Christian, and he's started taking their kid to church," Neil says.

A more extreme phenomenon, which we call the "divorce boomerang," also adversely affects some of the children of divorced interfaith parents, according to those we queried. An irate, about-to-divorce spouse who has made a commitment to raise the children in the other partner's religion may renounce his or her conversion, if any, and return to his or her birth culture. If the children are being raised "as both," the custodial parent may do her or his best to minimize the children's "other half," which represents the estranged spouse. In extreme cases, the "boomerang" parent yanks the children out of the religious culture in which they were being raised and marches them into the world of their "other half."

A recent, widely publicized example of a "boomeranger" is Kendra Avitan. Late in 1986, when the Toronto woman divorced her Orthodox Jewish husband, Meir, she began to take their infant son, Daniel, to Christian worship services. Contending that his former wife, a convert to Judaism, was violating a written separation agreement in which she had promised to raise the boy as a Jew and to feed him only kosher food, Meir Avitan fled to Israel with Daniel. Israeli courts returned the boy to his mother, a member of Jews for Jesus, and Daniel now attends a Christian nursery school in Ontario.

On trial for abduction, Meir Avitan told Toronto district judge David Humphrey, "To me it was a life-or-death situation. I could not let my son grow up a Christian." Ruling that there was no proof that Avitan knew of the court order restraining him from removing the child from Canada, Humphrey acquitted him of abduction charges. The father continues to fight for custody in family court.

With the sharp rise in weddings between Jews and Christians, within a few years we can expect to see many more children of failed intermarriages whose very identity will be used as a bargaining chip in the battle between their parents. As we saw in chapter 4, striking a comfortable balance between one's religious and ethnic cultures can be difficult even for those reared in relatively harmonious interfaith homes. How much more challenging it will be for the Daniel Avitans of the world!

Although not all divorcing interfaith spouses take sides, there's no way that the split can be painless. However, intermarried parents who refrain from insisting that the children go *their* way can ease the distress, as Justine explains. A secretary in her midtwenties who holds a degree in creative writing, Justine has shared both her father's cultural Judaism and her mother's New Age–influenced Christianity in the years since their marriage broke up. She remarks:

After my parents divorced when I was nine, I was asked to choose which parent I wanted to live with. I remember how devastating this was—choosing one meant rejecting the other. The same thing can happen if a child is forced to choose between Mommy's religion and Daddy's religion.

I lived alternately with each parent after that. When living with my mom, I participated in Om chanting, meditation, affirmations, and even a weekend Krishna retreat. From ages thirteen to sixteen, I lived with my dad and brother in a small town in which everyone but us was born-again Christian. . . . I have never forgotten the lessons of intolerance and bigotry that I learned in that Bible Belt high school.

I think children of an interfaith marriage should be exposed to both religions, but they should not be told, "This way is right, and that way is wrong." They should be allowed to experiment and to make their own decisions, but should not be pressured to choose.

Escaping relatively unscathed from her family's turmoil, Justine today enjoys a good relationship with both parents, which she attributes in part to the fact that "I was lucky enough to be raised without having to decide between two religions. My parents wisely allowed me to make my own choice." Today, Justine identifies with both Judaism and Christianity, but affiliates formally with neither.

Valerie was not quite as fortunate. A designer of instructional videos, she recalls, "My parents divorced when I was twelve. Though I was raised in a Jewish culture and knew no other identity, my Jewish grandmother hated my [non-practicing Catholic] mother for not being Jewish. I was very close to this grandmother, and always went to temple on the High Holidays and celebrated Passover with her." She adds that the divorce was traumatic for everyone, and the experience contributed to her emotional problems as a teenager.

In the face of divorce and remarriage, the concept of living between two worlds can become very real even for children raised in a virtually all-Jewish environment, as Valerie was, or as practicing Christians. Valerie and a number of other interviewees reported that after divorcing, their parents remarried and added to their extended families stepsiblings with a different religious orientation, or intensified their involvement with their birth cultures. After a Jewish woman became Valerie's father's second wife, for example, he became much more absorbed in Reform Jewish activities than he had been during Valerie's childhood. "My half-siblings are entirely Jewish by birth," says Valerie, "yet my sister does not seem to identify as a Jew, while my brother does."

Blended families whose members affiliate with different faiths are most prevalent by far among our youngest interviewees, demonstrating that in the future we'll see many more clans like Carolyn's. A student at an elite eastern women's college, Carolyn is the daughter of a secular Jewish man and an "all-American Baptist" woman. Reporting that her childhood exposure to both Judaism and Christianity was minimal, today Carolyn calls herself "an agnostic Jew with a Christian mother. I'm *especially* a Jew when I come across bigots." She remarks:

> I have two "real"—by which I mean biological—siblings, an older sister and a younger brother. They both consider themselves to be half-and-half, but I think they both identify more strongly with Judaism. I also have two stepbrothers by my stepfather who aren't Jewish, but they aren't really atheists either. They were just raised without religion.
>
> My stepmother's three children were raised Lutheran but went to Catholic school. My youngest stepbrother, a for-life Lutheran, jokingly identifies himself, through my father, as "step-Jewish."

Amid family turmoil, showing a strong preference for one parent, one faith, or a particular ethnic way of life may be asking for trouble. What happens when an interfaith couple makes a major change in their lives that's generally perceived as wholly positive—adopting a child?

Adoption. When interfaith couples adopt, yet more threads have to be woven into the family tapestry. The vast majority of adoptees who were raised in interfaith families are babies and small children, too young to complete our survey, even in Crayola. The reason for this is that prior to the 1970s, interfaith couples had a tough time adopting children at all, and few Jewish or Christian couples needed to adopt babies outside of their own ethnic groups. Limited access to safe and legal contraception and to abortion, as well as the stigma formerly faced by single women who wished to raise their children out of wedlock, guaranteed that a steady supply of babies would be surrendered to agencies run by Jewish and Christian groups.

Such organizations prefer to place infants with same-faith married couples, as Mischa, a former rabbinical student, confirmed. He said sadly that he and his Catholic wife had been told by the agencies they contacted that "a Jewish baby would never be given to a couple like us."

While their status as an interfaith couple obviously does not automatically make them unfit to adopt, it does complicate child rearing. Just as they must expend extra sensitivity and effort to deal with their very different backgrounds, adoptive interfaith couples must untangle a multihued skein of family ties: the husband's, the wife's, and the lineage of the adoptive child's birth parents.

According to writer Betty Jean Lifton, herself an adoptee, adoptive parents "should not panic: it does not stigmatize the adoptive family to recognize the inherent psychological dynamics in adoption. Nurturing an adopted child with empathy for her or his unique psychological needs is as important as milk and cookies."

Adult adoptees often feel that part of themselves is missing. They yearn to know more about their birth parents and their families, generally lack information about their birth parents' medical and family history, and may consider themselves "not as good" as other people.

In our opinion, the ordeals that the biological adult children and grandchildren of intermarriage undergo will be experienced *exponentially* by adoptees reared in interfaith homes. What we heard from the few adult adoptees we located who were reared by intermarried parents fills us with concern for their younger counterparts, who very likely will have to struggle mightily to achieve a sense of place in the Jewish and/or Christian communities.

Sophisticated Gertrude, a banker in her late forties, had this to say about her experience as an interfaith adoptee:

I consider myself to be a secular Jew, though I know very little about Judaism, because both of my biological parents were German Jews who disappeared in the Holocaust. At the end of World War II—I remember almost nothing about it—I ended up in an orphanage in Germany. My adoptive American mother, who was doing relief work in Germany, found me there.

My adoptive mother, who was a Christian married to a Jewish man, wanted to adopt a child, but agencies would not give children to older couples, and certainly not to a mixed couple. But she had such good connections because of her relief work that she was able to get me.

I can't say things worked out well. I was their only child. They loved me, of course. They gave me a lot. But my father became an alcoholic. After my [adoptive] mother died, I had to take care of him until he died. Then I went to look for my [biological] brother. I found him in West Germany. He hadn't been adopted, because at seven years my senior, he was too old. His life had been horrible, and he wanted me to save him, to take him to the United States and look after him. I just couldn't meet his demands, and finally I cut off all contact with him.

Acceptance problems for adopted children reared in interfaith and in Jewish homes go beyond the psychological problems common among other adoptees. The adopted children of a Jewish man who enjoys priestly or levitical status may not themselves become a *kohen* or *levi,* even after an Orthodox conversion, if their biological mother was born Gentile. As with any conversion, Orthodox Jews accept only halachic procedures; Conservative Jews, only Orthodox or Conservative conversions. And there are the preconceptions of the Jewish community to grapple with, as some of its members do not consider an adoptee, whether raised by two

Jewish parents or an interfaith couple, to be a "real" Jew. Brenda has experienced such discrimination firsthand.

Actress, writer, office worker, college professor, designer—she's worked at all these professions at one time or another. "I'm a rebel," Brenda says. "I've never held the same job for more than four years." Adopted by a Reform Jewish father, Brenda notes that her Catholic mother had converted to Judaism before adopting Brenda's older brother. "But here's where it gets complicated," says Brenda. "I only recently discovered that my biological mother was Catholic. I've had it out with a Conservative rabbi who told me to convert formally to Judaism. He said I wasn't really Jewish."

Although *she* considers herself Jewish, Brenda shares the ambivalence of other adoptees who were raised by interfaith parents, as Deborah does. A court reporter in her fifties, she notes, "Yes, I do feel as though I have 'two halves,' but that has more to do with my being adopted and wondering about my natural parentage." Born in the mid-1930s in Nazi Germany, Deborah was adopted by a Lutheran woman and a Jewish man. The family fled the Nazis, moving to Shanghai, China, where she attended a British-run Jewish school, before arriving in the United States. At the age of twenty-one, Deborah learned for the first time that not only was she adopted but that her biological mother had been Jewish, her father "Aryan."

Despite her halachically Jewish status, Deborah relates that her ex-husband's Jewish mother considered her a Gentile. Today, says Deborah, "I don't identify with any religious group, but consider myself a very moral person, culturally a Jew because that's who I am. I have never been interested in religion, and find them *all* hypocritical and damaging. It's not at all important in my life, one way or another." Her experiences as an adoptee also appear to have molded Deborah more definitively than has her upbringing in an interfaith home. And, like other Holocaust survivors we surveyed, Deborah's struggle for survival seems to have overridden many of the identity concerns voiced by other adult children of intermarriage.

Transcultural adoptions. Since so few healthy white infants—and so *very* few Jewish ones—are put up for adoption these days, Jewish and interfaith couples frequently look overseas for the children they plan to raise as Jews. (Many Orthodox Jews, in fact, prefer to adopt and convert a non-Jewish child, in order to lessen the possibility that as an adult, he or she will unknowingly marry back into their biological family.) Asian and Latin American babies fill many of these empty arms, according to Stars of David International, a support group for Jewish and interfaith couples who wish to raise their adopted children as Jews or in dual family heritages (see pp. 207–08).

Interfaith couples who adopt a child from a racial or ethnic group different from their own must be prepared to contend with subtle or blatant racism that may be directed at their child from members of any stratum of society, ranging from staring faces and inappropriate remarks to job and housing discrimination. In addition, if the adopted child is converted to Judaism, his or her parents must accept the fact that until the Jewish world becomes a tad more tolerant of ethnic diversity, their adopted child may be treated like a second-class citizen.

"Asian children raised by interfaith and Jewish adoptive parents tend to be received more warmly than the black adoptees," relates a Stars of David representative, who asked not to be identified. "Asian kids are considered cute, the black ones are—well, we haven't convinced the Jewish community that *they* are cute."

Multiculturality: A coat of many colors. If an adopted or biological child raised in an interfaith home possesses a racially mixed background, the family tapestry will indeed be colorful, but at times the threads may clash. Darlene, a social worker in her forties, says that her mixed status has been:

. . . the biggest pain in the neck. My complexion is kind of yellow, so everyone thinks I'm Puerto Rican or something. I have to keep explaining myself all the time.

My mother was an Orthodox Jew, and her family totally opposed her relationship with my [black] father. When I was born, they made her put me in foster care. Finally, when I was a year old, my parents said the hell with it, got married, and took me out of the foster home. At that point, my Orthodox family came around, and my grandmother taught me about *Shabbos*. I was raised as a Jew, and I still light candles every Friday night.

Darlene considers herself both black and Jewish, lives in a city that has a large black population, and counsels many racial-minority clients. Although comfortable in her dual identity, one issue still nagged at her: she had always felt that her Jewish family would have accepted her more readily if her father had been white. Robin's mother's family—once Orthodox, now Conservative Jewish—had welcomed her, had they not?

No, replied Robin, with the exception of her maternal Jewish grandmother. In fact, Robin believes that her stereotypically fair, "non-Jewish" appearance made her seem even more alien to her mother's dark, vivid relatives. This news appeared to upset Darlene deeply; only much later did Robin realize that she had deflated Darlene's "solution fantasy"— a concept we first explored in chapter 4. Darlene evidently believed that if her Christian father had been white rather than black, her mother's Orthodox family would more readily have considered her a "real" Jew.

The odyssey of black activist Julius Lester provides another example of the "solution fantasy" among interracial descendants of intermarriage. The great-grandson of a German Jew named Altschul and a black woman, Lester spent his Arkansas boyhood painfully aware that his father's house had many mansions, one of which he could not enter. As Lester has recounted in his memoir, *Lovesong: Becoming a Jew*, when he and his father would pass the store belonging to his white Jewish cousins, his father would tell him, "They're your blood relatives." He chuckled. "But don't you go marching in the store and call them cousin. They'd pretend like they didn't know what you were talking about."

As an adult, Lester converted to Judaism. When he finally sought out his white Altschul cousins, he appeared both surprised and amused to learn that they'd all converted to Christianity. Lester's private "solution fantasy" for his dual identity involved being accepted as a black Jew by his white Jewish relatives, a scenario rendered impossible by their departure from Judaism.

Not every descendant of interracial intermarriage has a "solution fantasy." Many manage to strike a bargain with their dual heritage, but not without a certain amount of attendant discomfort, wittily summarized this way by Washington, D.C., writer and musician James McBride, son of a white Jewish woman and a black man:

> Being mixed feels like that tingly feeling you have in your nose when you have to sneeze—you're hanging there waiting for it to happen, but it never does. You feel completely misunderstood by the rest of the world, which is probably how any sixteen-year-old feels, except that if you're brown-skinned like me, the feeling lasts for the rest of your life.

Jamal, another multiracial descendant of intermarriage, also views himself as "mixed, a real hodgepodge!" He adds, "I'm white/*black*/Hispanic/*Jewish*/Catholic, though what's underlined [italicized] is primary." The son of a white Jewish

man, Jamal explains that his mother's background is kalei-
doscopic, boasting black and Hispanic antecedents, as well
as one grandfather who was a white Sephardic Jew. A journalist and naval reserve officer, Jamal relates:

> There is a tendency on the part of some blacks and some
> Jews to believe that anyone who is a mixture is not part
> of the group, and to reject that person. I've also had some
> friends who question my commitment to my races and
> faith. Growing up in New York in the late '60s and having
> gone to Princeton—the WASPiest of all of the Ivy League
> schools—has given me the view that my mixed racial back-
> ground has had as much of a role in my life, if not more,
> than being of a mixed religious background.

Based on the experiences of a number of descendants of
stressed intermarriages, we offer the following suggestions
to others in their situation, as well as to the interfaith couples
currently struggling to cope with estrangement from relatives, divorce, stepparenting blended families, adoption, or
interracial living:

• **You have the power to reconnect with your lost "half."**
If, for whatever reason, you would like to learn more about
your Jewish and/or Christian extended families, see the tips
beginning on page 192.

• **Religious and ethnic differences probably weren't the
sole reason for your interfaith parents' divorce.** When intermarriages dissolve, the pain that the parents and children
experience is magnified when relatives and friends act as if
they've expected it all along, crowing, "So what do you
expect when you don't marry your own kind?" Comments
like these conveniently ignore the fact that endogamously
married Jews and Christians also divorce.

However, being intermarried probably *did* make it more
tricky for your parents to communicate. Vocal family and

communal opposition to their relationship may have magnified their feelings of isolation. "I have never felt that I was
living between two worlds, but my parents certainly perceived it that way," sympathizes Peter, who still appears
angry about how the Conservative Jewish congregation to
which his mother belonged treated his Catholic father. "My
parents were neither socially acceptable to their Jewish or
their Christian friends, or in their respective religious institutions," he adds.

Until the last few years, empathetic marriage counseling
specifically directed toward interfaith couples was very difficult to find. And, as we'll see in the following chapter,
spouses in a troubled intermarriage are so sensitive to the
doomsday predictions of hostile research studies and family
members that they may be reluctant to admit that any problems exist at all within the marriage.

If your interfaith parents divorced, it wasn't your fault,
and in any case, there's nothing you can do to alter ancient
history. But recognizing the issues involved can help us put
these failed marriages into saner perspective and make us
more comfortable in the here and now.

• **Think twice before surrendering one of your "halves,"
if your interfaith parents divorce.** If such a move seems
inevitable, or if the family broke up when you were too
young to exert any influence over the situation, remember
that you can always reclaim your lost heritage at a future
date (again, see the suggestions starting on page 192). No
statute of limitations governs your access. For a variety of
reasons, many children of divorced interfaith couples are cut
off from the ethnic and religious world of the noncustodial
parent, especially if he or she has a history of violence, sexual
abuse, alcohol or drug addiction, or has abandoned the
family.

While separating children from a parent's world may be
justified in extreme cases, it is important not to confuse a

parent's personal problems with his or her ethnicity. In one midwestern family, the children of a failed intermarriage heard their custodial Christian relatives repeatedly bad-mouth their father as "just a cheap Jew," because he rarely visited and sent child support only sporadically. The children came to regard their Christian stepfather as their "real" fa-ther for excellent reasons—he adopted, raised, supported, and loved them. But should they have been totally isolated, as they were, from all contact with the Jewish world, and exposed to anti-Semitic remarks, merely because their bio-logical Jewish father neglected his parental responsibilities?

• **If your divorced parent remarries, his or her religious and ethnic allegiance may change. It doesn't necessarily mean that yours will, too.** Becoming part of a blended in-terfaith family, in which the newly married husband and wife bring together their own children and complex back-grounds, is itself a stressful situation. The children, then, often feel they need to compromise their own identities in the interest of "fitting in." The question becomes, to what extent will you participate in rituals that are unfamiliar or unpalatable to you? What family traditions are you being encouraged to abandon? Just how far will you go in the interest of keeping the peace?

In order to maintain at least a modicum of harmony, in-terfaith blended families should strive to emphasize mod-eration in all things. Plan a Passover *seder*, for example, but don't insist that everyone present promise to convert to Ju-daism before the gefilte fish hits the table. Carve that Easter ham without remarking that everyone who hasn't accepted Jesus is going to hell. As many advisers to interfaith couples have noted, it is indeed possible to observe more than one religion in the home without stepping too brutally on one another's toes.

Interfaith parents who have switched religious or cultural allegiances upon remarriage ought not insist that their children—*of any age*—do so as well. As a child of interfaith marriage, the choice is yours to make, not your parent's or stepparent's. In extreme cases, pressuring a child to surrender one of his or her "halves" constitutes a form of spiritual kidnapping. If you are a teenager in this uncomfortable situation, and thus not yet in full control of your destiny, appeal to your other parent, rabbi, priest, clergyperson, or another sympathetic adult.

• **If you have been adopted by an interfaith family, you may find the advice in the following chapter to descendants of "runaways" particularly useful.** A "runaway" parent may discourage his or her child from learning more about the culture he or she abandoned and concealed upon marrying someone from a different background. But adoptive parents are even more skittish if their child begins to search for his or her birth parents. Interfaith couples have long been discriminated against by adoption agencies, and they may have waited many years for the opportunity to find and nurture you. Since any interest you might express in your birth parents may deeply threaten your adoptive family, please be low-key when you discuss the issue with them, as well as when you disclose to them any information you may glean in the process. If your adoptive family cannot or will not supply information about your birth parents, contact an adoptees' search group (see page 206).

• **Don't buy in to your adoptive interfaith parents' denial mechanism, if you feel it doesn't apply to you.** Even in same-faith, stable families, parents are often heartbroken when an adopted child plays second fiddle to his or her biological cousins. Grandparents may show hurtful favoritism toward their "real" grandchildren, since they cannot see "Lou's eyes" or "Penny's temper" in someone who is not related to them by blood. If the adopted child is non-Caucasian, the family will undoubtedly hear racist remarks; if the adoptive parents are of different faiths, that must be accommodated as well. In an attempt to block out negative external stimuli, interfaith adoptive parents are especially likely to present an "everything's fine" face to the world, minimizing the very real differences between the adopted child's birth culture and the world to which he or she now belongs.

Be patient with your adoptive parents, for they usually love you dearly and are as inextricably tied to you as any biological parent could be. But if they nourish the fantasy that adoption has erased the differences between your backgrounds, magically making yours the same as theirs, you probably will not be able to live out this daydream for them. You are—or should be—free to decide for yourself what you want and need to know about your birth parents' cultures, and to draw from as many worlds as you feel part of when building your sense of self.

• **If you're a descendant of a mixed-race Jewish-Gentile intermarriage, there's no need to drop either of your "halves," even if it placates your parents.** Interfaith parents who come from different races have had much to overcome in getting together and marrying in the first place. By the time the children come along, interracial parents are just plain *tired*, so they often try to ignore or gloss over the cultural differences between their ancestries, or they may resort to euphemisms by calling their children "tan," "mixed," "brown," or "multiracial," rather than "black and Jewish," or "Jewish and Puerto Rican." (Not all interracial parents evade the issue at hand so completely; for more information, see pages 206–07.)

At the risk of sounding like a broken record, we'll say it once again: If your parents are of different races as well as faiths, you come from *at least* two worlds, and *all* of them need you.

CHAPTER
8

Emerging from the Heart of Darkness— Survivors of Dysfunctional Interfaith Families

It is sad for me to have felt all my life that I haven't belonged anywhere. I think that feeling comes as much from my molestation as a toddler as it has from my family's refusal to talk about my roots—therefore, my *lack* of roots—and from my lesbianism. In a world that is dominated by the patriarchy and in a culture dominated by white Christian male values, how could I ever hope to feel that I belong anywhere, unless I can find that sense of belonging in myself?
—ELENA, ARTIST

My [Jewish] father has always been a very moderate drinker, but for years he became drunk on Christmas Eve and then didn't join us on Christmas morning. We were aware that he wasn't a part of Christian holidays.
—JOYCE, LEARNING DISABILITIES SPECIALIST

THE DYSFUNCTIONAL INTERFAITH FAMILY DIDN'T SOUND LIKE a very promising topic for the discussion group that Robin and I had formed for the adult children of Jewish-Gentile intermarriage. "Robin, other than you, who will dare to speak up about something like that in front of a room full of strangers?" I teased her.

At first, it had seemed unlikely that the well-fed, well-bred, well-behaved group members came from *those* kinds of homes. At previous meetings, they had spoken forcefully about how their status as descendants of intermarriage had complicated their relationships with their relatives as well as with the Jewish and Christian communities. Although nobody directly addressed more sensitive family problems, we sensed a note of underlying distress in some of the stories they told. So we scheduled a meeting on the topic of dysfunctional interfaith families, reasoning that even if only two or three people attended, they might find it valuable to air their grievances in a sympathetic setting.

Nine people arrived that spring evening. The atmosphere in Leslie's living room was suffused with a wary expectancy that we had not noticed during previous meetings. As we settled into our seats with coffee and cookies, Robin explained that her mother, who was subject to severe depressions, was a "runaway" who had concealed her Jewish heritage from her Christian husband and the four children she had raised as Episcopalians.

Regardless of religious and ethnic background, a parent or other family member's alcoholism, physical and/or verbal abuse, mental illness, or incestuous behavior will leave indelible marks upon the children of the family, who emerge ill-equipped to cope with the world, she said. But in a dysfunctional *interfaith* home, Robin added, the problems are complicated by the children's dual heritage, which may never have been addressed openly or constructively. Robin asked if anyone else in the room had a "runaway," depressed, alcoholic, or otherwise troubled parent.

Six hands were hesitantly raised. When Robin inquired gently if anyone would like to talk about their experiences, Debbie diffidently took the floor. Happily married to a Jewish man, Debbie now identifies as a Jew. But her present contentment is hard-won:

> My mother was a Jew who converted to Christianity. She didn't really want to be a Roman Catholic, but she did it in order to marry my father. My four brothers and sisters

and I were raised Catholic, and I went to Mass regularly.

My mother was very unhappy, and she began having nervous breakdowns when I was still a child. Since I was the oldest, I took care of the other kids when she was sick. She'd be all right for a while, and then there'd be another breakdown. When she'd go away [to be hospitalized], I'd be put in charge again. I never knew when it was going to happen.

As Debbie spoke, her eyes moistened, and for a moment her petite frame seemed to shrink, giving her the appearance of the frightened and exhausted child she must have been. Then others came forward, one by one, to speak. With passion, pathos, and intensity, the stories continued well into the evening.

In the years since that meeting took place, our research has revealed that Debbie and the others who spoke that night have plenty of company. Forty-one percent of the adult children and grandchildren of intermarriage whom we formally surveyed report that one parent, both parents, or another member of their immediate interfaith families had problems with alcohol and/or drugs, were subject to chronic mental illness, or were verbally, physically, sexually, or emotionally abusive. Alcoholism was the most frequently reported problem. While few respondents attributed these problems solely to their parents' intermarriages, a great many stated directly that they believed their family status exacerbated any dysfunction that happened to be present.

News like this falls very hard on the sensitive ears of interfaith couples—and rightfully so. Who wishes to believe that by falling in love and choosing a life partner, one's children may be placed in emotional jeopardy? However difficult it is to read the stories that follow, we ask you to stay with us. While we'll hear from individuals who were ravaged in body and spirit by their dysfunctional interfaith families, we have attempted to place their stories in an instructional context. In many cases, their problems could have been mitigated or forestalled altogether had their interfaith parents understood their family's unique position in society, and had they been able to find sympathetic, knowledgeable counseling within the Jewish and Christian communities.

Even in the absence of this kind of support and assistance, some of the survivors of dysfunctional interfaith homes whom we interviewed have triumphed over their problems and achieved serenity and balance as adults. From their stories of survival and change, descendants both of intermarriage and of interfaith couples who are starting new families can learn from the misunderstandings and errors of the past. Hard as the task may be at times, by expending extra effort and sensitivity, Jewish-Gentile couples can create a loving environment that respects the family's diversity and copes with budding problems. And it is never too late to benefit from self-healing and nurturing techniques, following the suggestions beginning on page 176.

In their efforts—whether forceful or feeble—to help themselves, troubled interfaith families are hindered by certain myths prevalent in both the Jewish and the Christian communities, voiced by clergy, counselors, and laypeople alike. Perpetuating these stereotypes actively fosters an airless, disapproving environment in which even emotionally healthy interfaith couples must work hard in order to raise well-balanced children.

Myth 1: Interfaith marriages are inherently dysfunctional, and the children of these unions are likely to be psychologically damaged. In a study published in 1968, Louis Berman went so far as to theorize that Jews who marry Gentiles are disproportionately motivated by neurotic influences. We do not espouse such a jaundiced view. Based on the childhoods

159

in two cultures experienced by hundreds of our fellow adult descendants, the issue proves to be considerably more complex than Berman's assessment.

Interfaith families are *not* dysfunctional in and of themselves, and even under stressful conditions they do not necessarily provide an abusive or traumatic environment. However, members of an interfaith family must expend more effort, in the form of patience, tolerance, and understanding, in order to make the family "work" than might be required from a household in which both spouses share a similar religious and ethnic background. At stake is not only the family's happiness but whether the children will perceive their dual identity as an asset or a liability.

In addition, unlike endogamous couples, spouses in a bicultural marriage cannot as easily coast along without making a special effort to teach their children about their twin heritages. If there are no relatives, neighbors, or friends nearby to help the interfaith parents provide their offspring with positive reinforcement of their status, the task becomes even more daunting. At this point, many interfaith couples bail out altogether, and, denying the difficulty of their mission, insist that their children's status is "no big deal."

Contemporary society offers few prominent, constructive role models for interfaith couples. The issue of intermarriage is often hopelessly trivialized by American popular culture, which is likely to emphasize only the piquant differences between the partners in such marriages. In one typically frothy magazine photo essay, for example, an intermarried pair of television actors showed off the Christmas tree and Hanukkah *menorah* arrayed side by side in their living room, but offered no clue as to how the family lives day to day (a little bit of Judaism, a little bit of Jesus, a little rock 'n' roll?), or how they choose to educate their children about their "two halves."

Newspapers present a flurry of articles every year on the

interfaith family's "December dilemma," as though the very real issues of faith and ethnicity are on display only as long as the holiday decorations (red and green? blue and silver? both?), after which the matter is retired for another year. While even a superficial treatment of this complex subject can help interfaith couples feel less isolated, it does little to alleviate the distress they may feel at having set up housekeeping in the face of parental and/or societal disapproval.

When serious problems such as alcoholism or physical abuse are piled atop the daily stresses of family life, even endogamous couples can be stressed to the limit. Factor in an interfaith couple's struggle to accommodate, in some fashion, two very different cultural heritages under one roof, and it's easy to see how the dysfunctional interfaith family may be pressured past the breaking point.

Myth 2: Only "bad" Jews intermarry. At least until one of their own, carefully reared children falls in love with a Gentile, some Jews still believe that only "bad" (*i.e.*, socially dysfunctional and religiously nonfunctional) Jews marry out of the faith. Our question is, were these Jews already "bad," or were they relegated to that status only upon intermarrying?

When pressed to define a "bad" Jew's background, a "born" Jew might distastefully describe a hypothetical secular or Reform—never Conservative or Orthodox—Jew with little or no religious education, who may have been actively dysfunctional (alcoholic, depressed, self-hating, violent) prior to his or her marriage. After hearing this argument any number of times, we could wearily summarize it as "nice Jewish kids don't marry out."

Wrong. Jews of *all* backgrounds have caused the rate of Jewish out-marriage to increase fivefold for men and twelvefold for women during the last generation. Among our interviewees, who were born in decades in which the intermarriage rate was far lower than it is today, 51 percent report that their Jewish parent was raised in a Conservative or Orthodox home. Almost without exception, these inter-married Jewish parents left Orthodox or Conservative Judaism as adults. Seventeen percent of our respondents say that they were raised as Jews, but not one was reared in an Orthodox home, and very few in Conservative Jewish settings.

Since Orthodox Judaism forbids intermarriage, and Conservative Judaism strongly disapproves of it, their members often sever their institutional ties upon marrying a non-Jew. This demonstrates why the intermarriage rate among the more traditional branches of Judaism may be severely underreported. Orthodox synagogues generally practice what one Orthodox rabbi termed, at a seminar we attended, "tough love," by ousting from membership or communally shunning any member who intermarries. A high expulsion rate among traditional Jews often accounts for an artificially low reported rate of intermarriage.

Myth 3: If child abuse occurs in an intermarriage, it is always carried out by the Christian spouse. This nasty anti-Gentile concept is simply not true. Of the questionnaire respondents reporting an abusive family background, some were molested or battered physically or verbally by a Jewish parent, some by a Christian parent, and others were unlucky enough to have been maltreated by both parents, and possibly by other extended family members as well.

Complaints from victims of family dysfunction are often silenced or muffled within the Jewish community on two grounds: reluctance to jeopardize the position of a family member within a tiny ethnic world, and the hesitance of the community to hear a victim's cries for help when something as unspeakable as sexual abuse, for example, occurs within a Jewish home. "Resistance to admitting that incest exists within the Jewish community apparently grows out of some mistaken claim that morally speaking, Jews are intrinsically different, and better—our generation's version of the claim that Jews do not drink and Jews do not beat their wives," confirms Rabbi Irving Greenberg, president of CLAL, the National Jewish Center for Learning and Leadership.

Researchers of Christian descent who study child abuse in Christian homes appear to express their horror and indignation more openly than do Jews studying abusive Jews. Denial doesn't serve the same protective function for Christians as it does for Jews. Christians collectively need not fear that disapproval will lead to wholesale oppression by a majority culture—they *are* the majority culture.

Myth 4: Children and grandchildren of Jewish men and Gentile women are not "real" Jews, and therefore should turn to the Christian community for help if they have any problems. Even if they are being raised as Jews, children of interfaith marriages who are not considered halachically Jewish may have difficulty obtaining treatment from Jewish social service agencies. In a 1973 study, Allen S. Maller examined 137 individual family units—30 of which were headed by interfaith couples—under treatment in a Philadelphia agency handling Jewish problem children. This office "has an understanding with the other local sectarian agencies not to accept each other's potential clients. Thus it will only accept the children of a Jewish mother," noted Maller.

Of the 30 interfaith couples studied by Maller, fully 80 percent comprised Jewish women married to Gentile men, whose children are presumed by the Jewish community to feel more comfortably rooted in Judaism than their patrilineal counterparts. Even though most of the interfaith couples he studied had produced matrilineal, "real" Jewish offspring, Maller concluded that children of mixed marriages were "about three times more likely to have severe emotional and behavioral problems than children from endogamous Jewish families."

Making matters even more difficult for troubled interfaith

families, a fair number of those who currently study or counsel them happen to be intermarried Jews or Christians. Their status as partners in interfaith marriages gives them vested personal and professional interests in presenting a relentlessly upbeat picture of intermarriage, and makes them reluctant to see *any* dysfunctions in a family that shares their status. Whereas the myths presented above depict interfaith family life in dreary shades of gray, intermarried researchers, therapists, and counselors often view interfaith family life through rose-colored glasses, as the following myth attests.

Myth 5: Interfaith couples seldom or never fall into dysfunctional behavioral patterns. Because they have had to expend extra effort in order to surmount their cultural differences, their homes are havens of humanistic warmth. We wish. Harmony is *not* a given within interfaith families, regardless of the obstacles that the interfaith couple may have had to overcome in order to marry—and stay married. Perhaps the tremendous increase in the intermarriage rate will usher in a brave new era as both the Jewish and Christian communities work harder to help interfaith families resolve their differences.

However, it may be twenty or thirty years before we learn what kind of adults are formed in the open, tolerant, flexible "peaceable kingdoms" pioneered by author Lee F. Gruzen and others who champion *productive* interfaith family life today. It is definitely too soon to assume that all the answers to bicultural living have been found, or that the needs of dysfunctional interfaith couples do not differ markedly from those of their dysfunctional, endogamously wed counterparts. Academicians and therapists studying interfaith family dynamics should ask the hard questions about abuse and dysfunction, in the hopes of expanding the all-too-small body of information on the subject. If they themselves are intermarried, they need to labor diligently to maintain their clinical detachment.

Since intermarried members of the academic community so often have a hard time acknowledging and accepting the particular vulnerability of interfaith families, one can imagine how difficult it is for the members of dysfunctional families themselves to admit that they may need help. Why? No one wants to hear a chorus of "I told you so!" from relatives, clergy, friends, and even counselors who disapprove of intermarriage. And friends and counselors who are intermarried themselves often want to hear only good news. Yet, as we'll see, there are many problems with which these families need professional help.

"No big deal" *redux.* In public, interfaith couples often assume a hearty, cheerful pose, in an effort to shield themselves and their children from potentially negative social feedback. *The number-one problem plaguing interfaith couples and their children and grandchildren, in our experience, is the rigid wall of denial that frequently gets erected, brick by brick, in an effort to shield the family from negative comments and to allow them to erroneously assert that their status as a religiously and ethnically atypical family is "no big deal."*

This phrase is voiced so frequently that counselors and researchers need to listen for it—without passing judgment—when interviewing members of interfaith families. Considering what they're up against, these individuals can hardly be faulted for trying to gloss over their differences. We were initially puzzled by the extremely normal appearance of some of the descendants of intermarriage that we met after founding Pareveh. If being the adult child or grandchild of an intermarriage was generally "no big deal," why were they giving up a precious weekday evening in order to attend a gathering sponsored by an organization whose support they claimed not to need?

However, once we began to ask quite innocuous questions about how they had been raised, had arrived at their spiritual beliefs, and what factors contributed to their interfaith families' harmony, the cheery facades of many of these descendants crumbled, as they haltingly confided what lay behind. In some cases, their families had tried to "block out" vicious treatment of their households by Jews, Christians, or both. Others revealed painful stories of family dysfunctions, ranging from verbal abuse to incest. The prevalence of such hidden traumas among dysfunctional interfaith families was corroborated in writing by those who responded to our questionnaire.

If a member of a troubled interfaith family has unconsciously adopted its "grand pretense" that no serious problems exist, he or she will strive diligently to deny the existence of *any* difficulties in his or her own life. It takes a lot of self-questioning in an environment in which one feels comfortable, which may involve psychotherapy, in order to crack the shell of such a person's denial, which began forming practically *in utero*.

While this denial is common even in stable interfaith homes, it has had a particularly damaging impact upon our respondents who say they come from dysfunctional families. They learn to put on a happy face at their parents' knees, as Leigh can attest. A housewife raising children of her own, she has labored mightily to break free of her "no big deal" behavioral patterns. For many years she asserted that the chaotic family she grew up in was as normal as Beaver Cleaver's, until her emotional and physical distress began to incapacitate her. She says:

Religion was supposed to be a nonissue in my home. My parents scoffed at "believers" of any stripe. I was aware very early that one of my parents had been born Jewish, the other, Gentile. When I asked, "What am I?", they answered, "Nothing. You're *nothing*." They insisted that their backgrounds didn't affect or identify them.

My parents have been alcoholics for many years, and I

was frequently abused physically and verbally by both of them until my late teens. They saw me as a burden, and took little interest in whatever was going on in my life, good *or* bad. During my childhood and adolescence, I was sexually molested by three people—two of them relatives— suffered from depression and migraine headaches, and had a difficult time getting along with other people.

I can't say that my status as a child of intermarriage is solely responsible for my poor beginning in life, or for the years of psychiatric repair work it has entailed. But my parents began their marriage by denying who they were, as well as how destructive their habits were to our family. The denial fed on itself, and permeated every part of our lives. Today, it's almost bigger than both of them.

The shield of denial worn by so many descendants of intermarriage mimics our interfaith parents' attempts to radically minimize their mutual differences and to shut out the opinions of outsiders who voice their opposition to intermarriage. This denial strategy may work for some of our parents, but its impact on us is wholly negative, *even in interfaith homes that are relatively peaceful and "successful."*

If the adult children of intermarriage are encouraged to believe, even in the face of contradictory evidence, that our interfaith families' bicultural existence is always an utterly positive experience, we will learn to doubt our intuitive feelings and instincts on many levels. In addition, high levels of denial in interfaith families encourage the development of two characteristic personality traits among their descendants, who may switch back and forth between what we've dubbed "dovish" and "hawkish" behavior.

Since we represent something of an experiment in bicultural living, the descendants of intermarriage most severely affected by family denial often appear as overly docile as white doves. These "doves of peace" exhibit an excessive desire to placate others, are eager to be considered normal, and go to pathetic lengths to conceal or minimize even modest eccentricities. "I guess it's all right if the Jews are mean to us. I mean, it's *their* religion, isn't it?" the daughter of a Jewish man and a Methodist woman once quavered to us.

Avram, an Orthodox Jew who is the son of a Gentile man and a Jewish woman, also exhibits a dovish desire to make peace, especially in all-Jewish or all-Christian circles. "I tend to hide my parentage from everyone, whether Jew or non-Jew," he says. "I prefer to conceal such a serious background flaw to prevent any possible misunderstanding in my life."

Family denial also can foster a highly reactive testiness, which is exacerbated in situations in which one parent was denigrated by members of the family's dominant culture. Children from such families often become "hawks," hypersensitive to rejection both by Jews *and* by Christians, and may express open hostility toward one or both parental cultures. Such descendants tend to downplay the importance of religious and ethnic institutions in general.

"I never expected that I would belong to *any* organized religion, though we were accepted as Jewish people in a predominantly secular Jewish community," says George, the son of a Catholic woman who converted to Judaism upon marriage. His Jewish father, says George, was "verbally abusive toward my mother. He rarely called her anything but 'stupid.' I am not close with him today, and I find it difficult to forgive him."

"Hawks" tend to go for the jugular. They frequently appear not to understand why achieving a sense of balance in one or more religious or ethnic identities matters so much to some offspring of interfaith marriages, and they sometimes scorn those who agonize over this issue. "I live a secular life, staying clear of both Christian and Jewish religions," says Parker, whose mother is Norwegian and Unitarian; his father is a Lithuanian Jew. Parker expresses his spiritual seeking through "nonreligious Tibetan sitting meditation, hatha yoga, and by taking outdoor walks." He adds:

> I believe the endogamy/exogamy nature of most religious organizations results in institutional entities that are primarily political, not spiritual, in nature. These divisive entities cause more harm than good for human society and the planet. I respect religious people who are tolerant and open to other beliefs and practices, but they are few and far between.

Motivating "hawkish" behavior may be a genuine anger at both the Jewish and the Christian communities for treating their interfaith parents tactlessly or negatively. These troubled adult children of intermarriage may be mad at Mom and Dad for getting them into this fix in the first place, or they may be turned off by pressures to affiliate with either parental culture.

"Hawks" appear especially likely to become completely estranged from both Judaism and Christianity and to turn to a third, unrelated spiritual path, as Damon has. Unmoved by his sister's conversion to Judaism or by his Protestant mother's ardent desire to see him choose Christianity, he calls himself "a mystic," and decisively severed himself from the traditions of his birth cultures, to the dismay of both parents.

"I didn't see that the church could help me find the deeper meaning in life I was looking for," says Damon, adding:

> I meditate, do yoga and *tai chi*, and run on the beach in the morning. I read the spiritual masters, most recently Gurdjieff and Meher Baba, and went to see Yogi Amrit Desai at a retreat recently. I consult the *I Ching* regularly. I live an ascetic simple life and try to follow the Eastern way of detachment.

Descendants of intermarriage often vacillate between "dovish" and "hawkish" behavior, tending toward meekness in public, fury in private and among trusted friends. Whether reticent or enraged, these descendants of intermarriage are especially likely to be annoyed if they have overcome troubled childhoods and made strenuous efforts to be accepted in a particular religious or ethnic culture, only to be met with rebuffs. "When I first started trying to get involved with the Jewish community, once people found out that my mother is Gentile, I was often asked why my parents had gotten married in the first place. It's not as if I had any control over that," Leigh says with exasperation.

A wealth of contemporary literature addresses alcoholism, child abuse, and other family troubles; these books detail how survivors of dysfunctional home environments can mend the damage and move on. Such problems become even more complex in interfaith homes. An intermarried couple that already is having trouble integrating their very different backgrounds into a reasonably harmonious family life may be stressed beyond endurance by such common dysfunctions as substance abuse and mental illness, creating a terrifying environment for their children.

Victoria, a business executive, remarks that her alcoholic Christian mother used her daughter's status as a child of intermarriage "as a tool to keep me from fitting in . . . At Jewish day camp, I was half-Christian; at Christian school, I was half-Jewish. She told *everyone*." Yet, Victoria's mother had told her that she could choose her own religious identity when she grew up, and Victoria did just that. When she married a Jew and decided to identify as Jewish, Victoria says, "Mom *hated* the idea, and feels that she lost somehow." She was so enraged, in fact, that she badgered her daughter with "abusive, threatening" telephone calls until "we had her arrested and dried out for a while," Victoria relates.

Remorse over one's decision to marry out may be magnified dangerously if an intermarried parent has a substance-abuse problem. Carey's alcoholic mother, married to a Jew, "was determined to make me a Catholic. Otherwise, she feared that I would burn in hell," Carey remarks, adding that although she has always identified as a Christian, the "pressure and constant pulling toward Catholicism" persisted until her mother's death. "Certainly my mother's guilt about marrying outside her faith, coupled with her alcoholism, contributed to her suicide and many of my own tough growth periods," she says.

Today, at fifty, Carey says she feels at peace with herself. "Co-dependency is part of my life that I am working through. I've worked hard to overcome whatever problems my two worlds have presented me. I think it has made me a stronger and more thoughtful person," she reflects.

Carey has taken her lemons and made lemonade, but like other descendants of dysfunctional interfaith homes, she's found it difficult. Although longing passionately for security and order, these survivors may perpetuate the unhappiness of their childhoods by unconsciously creating melodramatic situations within their personal and work lives, a phenomenon known as "excited misery." Survivors of dysfunctional families, sustained for years on the adrenaline that surges as they cope with frequent emergencies, often are unable to construct orderly adult lives for themselves until they enter therapy or join a Twelve-Step program, such as Adult Children of Alcoholics.

"Runaways." Faced with the already difficult task of integrating two cultures into one home, some interfaith parents bail out from their birth cultures altogether, becoming what we've termed "runaways." Ten percent of the individuals we formally queried disclosed that one parent or grandparent cut all ties with their birth culture (usually Judaism), and thereafter concealed their former identity, whether partially or fully. Many of these descendants of intermarriage did not

171

discover the true background of their "runaway" relative until after they'd reached adulthood.

Whenever the truth reveals itself, an individual who learns that a parent or grandparent left his past behind generally finds that bald fact less upsetting than the deception itself. Half a century has passed since Rena learned her mother's true identity. Yet Rena, now in her sixties, still appears too distressed about her parents' trickery. Although she was never baptized, Rena's mother had joined a Congregational church at her husband's request. When Rena was eleven, her mother finally told her about her "old-country, Yiddish-speaking Orthodox Jewish family":

> I felt dirty upon finding out that I too was one of those awful people I had heard so much about. . . . At first I was ashamed of being half-Jewish, but at about age seventeen I became interested in Jewish issues. In my first year of college, at Barnard, I surreptitiously attended Jewish student activities.

Runaway parents vary in the degree to which they become invisible to their birth cultures and to their adopted cultures. Some cut nearly all family ties and never confide their true status to anyone during their lifetimes. Others get by in their adopted communities by saying as little as possible about their backgrounds, and by swearing their children to secrecy. Runaways have a wide variety of reasons for going underground. A relatively clear-cut rationale is advanced by the interfaith families that have opted to withhold information about a spouse's heritage solely to ensure the family's economic survival, as was the case with Joyce's father. His separation from the Jewish faith began at the age of thirteen, when the Depression wrenched his family from its economic security and its community, she explains. He was forced to leave school, and after years of struggle, he established himself professionally in a small, exclusively Christian southern town.

In the mid-1950s, when her parents had three children under the age of six who had already been baptized in the Presbyterian church, Joyce relates, "my father felt an impetus to make a religious change so that our growing family could fit in." He joined a Methodist church shortly before moving to a new town, in which his self-Anglicized surname would not arouse suspicion about his antecedents. When Joyce was twelve, her father admitted to her that he was Jewish. She notes:

This revelation was prompted by the upcoming visit of my cousins. My father surmised that I was bound to discover that our last names were not the same and that we had very different lifestyles. My father's demeanor was deadly serious when he announced, "Joyce, I want to see you in your room." I felt certain that I was about to be reprimanded for something.

Although I knew little of the Jewish religion and knew no Jewish people, I was dumbfounded by this news that was dropped in my lap. My father seemed tense and uncomfortable as he talked. The most damaging aspect of this encounter was his admonition that I was never to tell anyone. He tried to explain this rule of silence by saying that the people in our community wouldn't understand, and suggested that his livelihood might be jeopardized.

He was probably right, and I can appreciate the fact that he was trying to protect us. But at the age of twelve, I was reeling with questions of why—why would anyone object to my father? He was a kind and respected man. Why were we living around people who might object to us?

Somehow, my father's injunction against disclosing this information within my childhood community had a powerful silencing effect on me. I felt that my revealing my status as a child of intermarriage would be nothing less than a slap in my father's face.

As an adult, Joyce divulged her dual heritage for the first time to her oldest friend, who was shocked. "She kept saying, 'Joycie, how could you never tell me?' I felt just as puzzled as she about my ability to withhold this information from her. In deference to my father's feelings, I was capable of acting very uncharacteristically."

Globetrotting photojournalist Margaret Bourke-White is a prominent example of how an adult child of intermarriage may struggle to come to terms with a runaway parent. According to biographer Vicki Goldberg, Bourke-White's father, Joseph White, was raised in a strict Orthodox family whose children, as they reached adulthood, "introduced rationalism, skepticism about the Orthodox religion, and Ethical Culture into the home."

Neither Judaism nor religion in general meant much to White. During his engagement, he wrote to his fiancée, Minnie Bourke, "I have no regrets in saying that I will do my share in dissipating the race. . . . It will find better field if merged into the American spirit, American virtue, of the regenerating American type." For all his self-professed forthrightness, he embraced Ethical Culture and "kept his religion hidden," while Minnie Bourke "was calmly anti-Semitic," according to Goldberg. Bourke-White did not discover her mixed heritage until she was a young adult, and Goldberg called it:

> . . . a secret that gnawed at her mind and threatened to topple what equilibrium she had left. . . . Either the knowledge gave her an early sense of shame or her mother passed the shame on with the dark secret. Margaret's love for her father was boundless, yet she must have felt he

bequeathed her a flawed heritage. All her life she would be expert at covering up flaws; this one she covered over with special care.

In 1923, Bourke-White finally told her secret to her psychiatrist. The notes in her diary are brief: "Told the dr. Father was a Jew. He amazed—thinks it at the base of my inferiority complex—that I will now improve," quotes Goldberg. In fact, Bourke-White's mental anguish did ease. Her doctor "found her so improved that he cut back the number of her visits. Her secret was no longer poised to crush her life."

Bourke-White may have reached a very private kind of peace with her dual heritage, but it was not a fact she chose to make public. When Bourke-White's autobiography, *Portrait of Myself*, was published, an English-Irish grandmother was mentioned, but the book "never breathed a word about a grandfather named Weiss," says Goldberg.

The secrecy and denial that permeate families like Robin's, Rena's, Joyce's, and Bourke-White's are, unfortunately, common in interfaith families that harbor a runaway, descendants of intermarriage say. It may take years for a troubled individual to detect how life with a runaway parent may have magnified his or her own distress. One psychiatrist told us:

I have a patient who has a number of very pressing problems in her life, but she kept insisting that there was one thing that she really, really couldn't talk about. Finally, at one session, her voice dropped to a whisper, and she told me that she had found out that her mother had been Jewish. For months, I'd been imagining all kinds of unspeakably lurid stuff that she couldn't bring herself to admit, and it turned out to be *this*. It was clearly very upsetting to her.

While runaway behavior varies in severity, the emotional impact upon the interfaith parents, their children, and their grandchildren is unquestionably negative. While some descendants of intermarriage may show deep understanding of why a parent or grandparent chose to bolt from his or her birth culture, not one person we queried appears to approve of the action.

Descendants of intermarriage who have a runaway relative are in a position similar to that of adoptees who wish to know more about their biological parents. "No matter how good their adoptive experience, most adoptees feel an impaired sense of identity that comes from being cut off from knowledge of their origins—a human need and a human right," notes Betty Jean Lifton, the author of two books on the subject. Like adoptees, descendants of runaways may feel vaguely incomplete, as though part of them is missing. Once they learn of their dual status, they may embark on emotional, expensive, and prolonged searches for their "other half."

However we affiliate, we must sort out the religious and cultural complications presented by our dual heritage, a task that is made infinitely more difficult if we came of age in dysfunctional homes. That's the bad news. With pride and excitement, however, many of the survivors of dysfunctional interfaith homes have told us how they're progressing away from the negative patterns imprinted during their formative years. So can you, if the shoe fits . . . Here's how to get started:

• **If your family is dysfunctional, remember that your parents' or grandparents' intermarriage is not solely responsible for the situation.** Plenty of endogamously married Jews and Christians drink too much, beat, molest, or verbally abuse their children, too. However, your parents' or grandparents' status as an interfaith couple probably did make it more difficult for you and other family members to admit that a problem might exist and subsequently to seek help. Maintaining a dysfunctional interfaith family's "grand pretense" of normalcy benefits no one. Rather, it's a sign of strength—*not* of weakness—to concede that someone or something in your family is affecting you adversely, and to seek help to resolve the situation to your satisfaction.

• **You can only work on yourself.** If your progress influences others in your family, well and good. But don't count on it, and avoid crusading to reform anyone else. If it seems appropriate, share what you've learned about yourself with other family members, but don't be surprised if they accuse you of making a big fuss about nothing. Having a parent who is emotionally disturbed, is a substance abuser, or abuses *you* is hardly "nothing."

If your family responds defensively to your desire to grow and change emotionally, don't waste your time trying to break through their denial and force them to see the situation as you see it. By your quiet, positive example you may encourage them to change as well; at the very least, they may come to realize that you are dead serious about living your life differently. Consequently, they may be less inclined to continue their old patterns of abuse—with you, at least.

• **Both personally and professionally, don't let your dysfunctional interfaith parents "move in" with you.** If your Jewish father abused you verbally, do you unconsciously seek out Jewish men who do the same? Are you married to a blowsy Irish rose who drinks like your alcoholic Catholic mother did? The destructive patterns learned early in a dysfunctional interfaith family need not continue to dominate and even destroy your life. Just because a situation is *familiar* to you does not mean that it is appropriate. Many survivors of chaotic families instinctively enter into bad relationships as adults because comfort and contentment feel so alien. It may seem less threatening to remain negatively linked to one's past than to break away to start anew. Believing oneself to be unworthy of happiness is a common legacy of life in a dysfunctional home. Break the chain. You deserve it.

 • **If you can, and when you can, try to forgive your dysfunctional interfaith family members.** A number of contemporary psychologists set great store by forgiveness, simplistically claiming that by pardoning those who trespass against us, hurt feelings will magically heal, and hideously unbalanced relationships will be resolved, just like that. We take a more cautious approach. Certainly, dysfunctional family members should not be allowed to continue abusing or exploiting you, whether or not you've "forgiven" them. Forgiveness doesn't mean that you can never confront them about their past misdeeds. It doesn't mean trying to suppress your bad memories at all costs. But if your abusive relatives say they're sorry, and if they're clearly sincere, and if they are making even small, tentative efforts to recover, consider giving them the chance to reenter your life.

 • **Cut your losses by accepting them.** Some dysfunctional interfaith family members will stubbornly cling to their habits until they die. They won't stop abusing you *or* themselves, and they will not surrender their addictions. You may feel that the only way in which you can preserve your fragile emotional health is to distance yourself completely from an abusive parent or other relative. Coming to such a decision is excruciating, no doubt about it. But if all possibilities for reconciliation have been exhausted, it may be the only workable option.

If you decide—optimally, with the help of a counselor—that you must sever your ties with some members of your family, consider leaving a window open. Stay in touch with a sibling who's on speaking terms with your parents, for example. Phone your estranged brother's kindly secretary every few months. In time, your relatives may experience a change of heart. But if they don't, remember that it is not your responsibility to change their unacceptable behavior.

• **If you have a runaway relative, move slowly and cautiously when trying to enlighten yourself about his or her past.** Your situation is similar to that of an adoptee who is looking for his or her birth parents. Before contacting relatives whom you have never met, consult books about or by adult adoptees and visit an adult adoptees' search group (see page 206).

When making initial contact with your "missing" family members—by mail is the least stressful—tell them about yourself and enclose a photograph. Suggest an initial meeting at the home of a family member known to both of you, whose judgment they trust. If you seem comfortable together, gradually get to know the rest of the family. Since many of us who have runaway relatives fervently crave their approval and acceptance, we may be tempted to vow immediately to convert and to live as they do. Go slowly. Take classes in their religion and culture, study it carefully, talk to sympathetic clergy, and make sure that you could live comfortably within that world.

If you're received cordially by your missing family, and can sustain a relationship with them, that's certainly reason to rejoice. It will provide you with the opportunity to nurture the relationships that you've always longed for and will give you a greater understanding of the two worlds into which you were born. But if these newly found relatives are not interested in getting to know you, or if they withdraw after initial contact, don't blame yourself. Be grateful to the fates that you were able to find them in the first place. Even if you despise one another on sight, a negative experience can be just as instructive as a positive one. These relatives have permitted you a brief glimpse behind a door that has always been tightly barred to you—and that's better than nothing.

• **Be tactful, of course, but don't let your runaway parent or grandparent talk you into abandoning your search for their relatives.** Even if abuse or neglect compelled the runaway to move on, the people who harmed him or her just might have undergone a change of heart, or they may have died. It's possible that the family members who remain are people you'd like to get to know.

Despite your intense curiosity about your missing relatives, don't forget to reassure the family you've always had. They may panic as you begin to search for the kinfolk they left behind. They may be afraid they'll lose you to a heritage that may now seem utterly foreign to them, since years have elapsed since they chose to abandon it. No matter how the descendants of runaways ultimately opt to affiliate, they need to retain their emotional ties to the family members they first came to know. You'll always belong to two worlds, and both of them need you.

• **Are you part of the problem?** Do you, as a descendant of a dysfunctional intermarriage, drink too much? Feel like an angry "hawk" much of the time? Has depression become the norm in your life? Are you a passive "dove" who feels responsible for meeting everyone's needs but your own? Don't be too hard on yourself for answering "yes" to any of these questions, for no one escapes unscathed from a dysfunctional family. Although you can repair yourself through trial and error, without expert advice it probably will take longer to achieve the results you desire. Ask your physician for a referral to a well-regarded mental-health professional.

• **Forgive yourself, too.** Maybe you've done things as an adult that you're not proud of. Lacking control in our chaotic early lives, many descendants of dysfunctional families feel that we simply cannot take a wrong step, or all of our hard-won equilibrium will be lost. When you begin to berate yourself for your perceived inadequacies, step back, take a deep breath, and ask yourself, "Can we talk?" If you are comfortable with the idea, pose the same question to God. "The Lord God is merciful and gracious," says the Reform

Jewish liturgy for the Sabbath of Repentance, "endlessly patient, loving, and true, showing mercy to thousands, forgiving iniquity, transgression, and sin, and granting pardon."

If God can forgive us, maybe we can pardon ourselves—and others. We don't show true humility or forgiveness by endlessly flagellating ourselves for our weaknesses, failures, mistakes, and sins. Nor is it necessary to keep lashing out at our dysfunctional interfaith parents and relatives, or to seethe in silence, if it becomes clear, after sincere efforts to talk with them, that they cannot or will not shoulder part of the responsibility for our ongoing distress and work toward repairing their damaged relationships with us.

We simply need to admit to ourselves, without rancor, that our parents are not perfect, and neither are we. We made mistakes today, and we'll make some more tomorrow. Bit by bit, day by day, we can work to eliminate the negative habits that nourish our weaknesses, as we learn to nurture and cherish *both* of our "halves." Energized by our newfound self-acceptance, we can go forth to love ourselves and others better than we ever could before.

9

What Others Can Do to Help Us, Individually and Institutionally

Being from two or more worlds isn't such a terrible thing. In fact, if anything, it's a special blessing. What I may lack in a simple, regulated life—one religion, one ethnic background—is more than compensated for by the richness of my family's lives in different countries and religions.

—TRINA, LEGAL SECRETARY

I have several—many—friends who are married to non-Jews but are raising their children as Jews, or at least instilling a Jewish identity in them. Perhaps intermarriage between Jews and Gentiles should be retaught in a more positive light that will strengthen Judaism rather than weakening it. I think this must be done if the third generation is to maintain a Jewish identity.

—LINDSEY, WRITER

THE JEWISH HIGH HOLY DAYS ARE ALSO KNOWN AS *YOMIM Noraim,* the Days of Awe. One year we were awestruck indeed—simply by hearing one rabbi's harshly voiced opinion of intermarriage.

Seated in the sanctuary, we were carried along on a peacefully rolling tide of Hebrew liturgy that Rosh Hashanah morning. Friends greeted one another in low voices. Children wandered in and out, pausing bashfully before an elderly couple who can be counted upon to distribute generous handfuls of sweets from a bulging velvet *tallis* bag that holds plenty of candy as well as a prayer shawl. We felt rightfully placed, part of a community we had freely chosen.

It was comforting to be there as unobtrusive worshipers, rather than as obvious reminders of controversy. When we address Jewish groups as representatives of Pareveh, our status as adult children of intermarriage precedes us. The audience scrutinizes us painstakingly. Do we look like Jews? Are we on secret assignment from a Christian missionary group? Do we represent an active threat to the Jewish people, or a welcome addition? On this second day of Rosh Hashanah, we were happy to focus our minds on broader issues than our status within the Jewish community.

Or so we thought.

When the rabbi rose and began his sermon, our sense of spiritual ease and solidarity quickly drained away. Delivering a sort of State of the Jewish Union Address, the rabbi chided the congregation for failing to give money to Jewish causes, to support Israel, and to spend time on Jewish observances— the usual High Holy Day harangue, as any Jew can tell you. But the rabbi finished off by disclosing how high the intermarriage rate had risen in several cities, implying that interfaith couples held the power to annihilate Judaism. As the congregants began to murmur excitedly, the rabbi's face pulled into a tight, V-shaped smile of satisfaction. He had made his point—erroneously, perhaps, but sharply honed nonetheless.

We wondered when we'd ever cease feeling as though we had to apologize to the Jewish community for our very existence. Born-Jewish friends to whom we later recounted this experience tried to mollify us by saying that the rabbi was attacking intermarriage in the abstract, as a phenomenon. "He wasn't talking about you *personally*," they'd say.

It's true, we weren't addressed by name, but the rabbi's sermon demonstrated how easy—and unconstructive—it is to perpetuate such a negative vision of the descendants of intermarriage. When speaking before an audience already uneasy about the implications of marrying out of the faith, it's tempting to portray the members of interfaith families as a sinister, faceless army, marching in lockstep on an unstoppable mission to destroy Judaism. Actually, in the absence of institutional understanding of our unique status problems, the descendants of intermarriage are forced to maintain a fiercely independent approach to identity, as individual as our fingerprints. Our path toward our spiritual homes—whether Jewish, Christian, or neither—needs to be cleared, not cluttered further.

The pull toward Judaism in particular needs to be facilitated, as Christianity is more accommodating of newcomers and in recent history has seen few impediments to its growth. Since all denominations of Christianity work energetically to attract the spiritually uncommitted, America's dominant religious culture needs little advice from us on outreach. Our fuzzy status also appears to be a less crucial issue to Christian-identified descendants of intermarriage, primarily because Christianity has just a few clear-cut admission requirements: All adherents must freely choose Jesus as their Savior, renounce any previous religious practices, and be baptized.

A shorter "wish list." Not only must they clear fewer hurdles in order to participate fully in their chosen spiritual communities, but Christian-identified descendants of intermarriage who are satisfied with their choice have a shorter "wish list" than do their Jewish counterparts. They tell us they'd like to see a greater appreciation of their Jewish background within their churches, an end to anti-Semitism, and tolerance for their Jewish and secular relatives who are unmoved by Christian evangelism.

In return, they want their Jewish and secular family members to accept their pull toward Christianity without seeing it as a barb deliberately cast at their hearts. And since Christian-identified descendants of intermarriage feel that their shared Old Testament antecedents link them to Judaism, they'd like to be viewed by the Jewish community as comrades rather than as turncoats.

This is quite a lot to ask of a culture that traditionally has been loathe even to consider a Jewish-identified child of a Jewish father and Gentile mother as a "real" Jew, much less accept the Christian-identified descendants of intermarriage as potential allies. Yet, the Jewish community needs all the potential members and friends it can get. To find them, for starters, it need look no further than among the adult children of intermarriage, both matrilineal *and* patrilineal.

"All or nothing at all." Patrilineals are particularly vulnerable to Judaism's "all or nothing at all" attitude about Jewish identity, since, unlike matrilineals, they are not automatically considered "real" Jews by many "born" Jews. This inflexible definition erects needlessly high barriers before the spiritually ambivalent descendants of intermarriage, who'd like to come in and browse for a while before buying, or who are willing to lend their voices, hearts, and checkbooks to Jewish activities even if they eventually choose not to affiliate as Jews.

Given the general negativity that confronts descendants of intermarriage who consider identifying as Jews, it is amazing that although just 17 percent of our respondents report that they were raised as Jews, 44 percent identify as Jews today. And some of our respondents who identify as Christians, as "nothing," or who lead a secular life were raised as "real" Jews, and switched allegiances as adults.

Of the 27 percent of our respondents in the "nothing," secular, or "half and half" affinity group, a good many express feelings toward Judaism that are at best neutral, at worst quite negative. Many of these individuals appear bruised by what they perceive as the harshly judgmental attitude of the Jewish community toward their parents' intermarriage and their own nebulous status—*even if they are matrilineal descendants of intermarriage.*

While we understand the implacability of *halacha*, which accepts as "born" Jews only the children of Jewish mothers, it is ironic that so many non-Orthodox Jews, who comprise nine-tenths of American Jewry, cling so tenaciously to just this one aspect of *halacha*, while discarding so many other laws—such as those governing *kashrut, taharas hamishpachah,* and strict Sabbath observance—that they consider irrelevant to their own lives.

Even among secular and not-particularly-observant Jews, an ironclad insistence upon conversion for the children of Jewish men and Gentile women who seek to live Jewishly often overshadows all other Jewish population issues. Patrilineals frequently are not taken seriously by a Jewish community that behaves as though there's no need to educate us about our Jewish "half" unless we humbly agree to commit ourselves fully to Judaism as soon as we make its acquaintance, as well as hide our Gentile "half" away so that it will not discomfit Jewish eyes. And Reform and Reconstructionist Judaism's official acceptance of the children of either Jewish fathers or Jewish mothers is not as all-inclusive as it first appears. If these individuals are not raised as Jews *from birth*, depending on the situation and the tolerance of a particular rabbi or congregation, they may be required to convert formally as adults, Jewish mother notwithstanding.

Such an emphasis on conversion makes it seem as if ambivalent descendants of intermarriage are asked to promise, "Yes, of course I'll marry you," as soon as we shyly initiate a flirtation with the Jewish community. Especially if we were raised as Christians or as "nothing," descendants of intermarriage and the Jewish community need to get to know one another in a thousand ways, great and small, before a formal commitment can be made.

Halacha notwithstanding, many patrilineal descendants of intermarriage consider conversion unnecessary, yet something we may choose to undergo simply in order to make other Jews more comfortable with us. Patrilineals often chafe not at the halachic requirement that we convert to achieve full status in the Jewish community, but at the assumption that we represent a blank slate waiting to be inscribed with the basics of Jewish life, as though we had no Jewish ancestry or experience whatsoever. The patrilineals' aggravation in this regard may be shared in the near future by secularly or Christian-raised matrilineals who, in certain circumstances, may find that they must convert in order to be fully accepted by Reform and Reconstructionist congregations.

For most patrilineals we talked to who've decided to go ahead and convert, the process serves more as a public assertion and confirmation of our *existing* beliefs, conferring greater importance to our Jewish "half," rather than symbolizing a sea change from a totally Gentile life to a Jewish one.

Perhaps it would be more constructive, and not in violation of *halacha*, to consider conversion merely one step along the continuum of a Jewish life. "Real" Jewish status may be necessary before we undergo a life-cycle ceremony or are called to the Torah for an *aliyah* (chanting the blessings before and after the Torah reading), for example. But conversion should *not* be viewed as a ticket of entry that must be earned before we can begin to feel at home within Judaism. Conversion actually may prove anticlimactic for the descendants of intermarriage who've gone through the process, many of whom report that the strongest emotion the ceremony evoked in them was relief, i.e., "Now I can get on with the business of being Jewish, without all those explanations."

"The few, the proud . . ." Even after a formal commitment to Judaism, whether made for us as infants or actively undertaken by us as adults, Jewish life is not without ongoing pain and conflict, say a number of Jewish-identified descendants of intermarriage we've queried, matrilineal as well as patrilineal. They remark plaintively that rather than offering them a quarrelsome-but-loving extended family, the Jewish community seems more like the Marine Corps, with its stiff admission standards, intense scrutiny of new recruits, and its subliminal message: *We're looking for a few good Jews.*

What is a "good" Jew? Who decides? The definition varies from individual to individual, rabbi to rabbi, group to group, *shul* to school. Descendants of intermarriage who choose to live as Jews often need thick skins and a mulish stubbornness in order to remain in a camp that frequently views us as marginal members at best. As walking evidence of how many Jews choose Gentile mates, we serve as lightning rods for the unease that the Jewish community feels about its future. Considering that the descendants of intermarriage are likely to comprise the majority of American Jews by the year 2030, is such skepticism about our intentions "good for the Jews"? We think not.

Any disapproval that a Jewish-identified descendant of intermarriage faces from co-religionists is particularly hurtful in light of how far the Jewish community bends over backward to entice unaffiliated "born" Jews into greater involvement with educational, religious, and communal activities. If a secular, endogamously reared Jew becomes more observant after a lifetime of apathy, he is greeted joyfully and without stigma as a *ba'al teshuvah* ("one who has returned"). However, even a good many *matrilineal* descendants of intermarriage report that at some point in their lives, they were the unwilling recipients of free-floating Jewish hostility about their parents' or grandparents' decision to intermarry, or have been viewed as only marginally Jewish. (This may explain in part why just 52 percent of our matrilineal, "real" Jewish respondents live as Jews today, not close to 100 percent, as the Jewish community would mistakenly surmise.)

Complicating our transition to Jewish life, if that is how we choose to affiliate, is the fact that nobody can agree on how to calibrate a yardstick that would definitively determine "who is a Jew." Even when emotion gives way to a cool-headed gathering of statistics, the markings on the yardstick blur. Estimating the Jewish population is "not an exact science," say the authors of the *American Jewish Yearbook*, who remark that the growing number of intermarriages has made the task more difficult. "It's difficult to determine who really counts," says Jeffrey Schnecker of the North American Jewish Data Bank. Many communities, he adds, have begun tabulating separate lists of "real" Jews and of members of interfaith families who live in homes with some connection to Jewish life.

It's nice to see at least a cursory nod toward people who are not considered 100 percent Jewish but have a tie to Jewish life that may be profound. For anyone with a Jewish parent or grandparent, our Jewishness is like that red wool sock that somehow ends up in the load of white laundry: it colors everything it touches. Whether we're tinted a delicate pink or shrieking crimson, whether we're Lutheran or Lubavitcher, we'll always carry at least part of that red sock, that Jewishness, within.

The strength and flexibility that our link to two worlds provides is perhaps the greatest advantage of our mixed status. The vast majority of people we've queried over the past few years state proudly that a dual heritage provides a broader understanding of both birth cultures, a greater acceptance of the ambivalence that is an inevitable part of life, and increased tolerance for the beliefs and opinions of others. Yet we often pay a high price in order to enjoy these benefits.

Descendants of intermarriage frequently admit that they are likely to remain observers, outsiders, who feel they can never truly belong to either the Jewish or the Christian world. Regardless of how they affiliate, or would like to, 53 percent of our respondents say that it has been difficult or impossible to find a spiritual community within which they feel comfortable. This inability to connect frequently extends beyond our interest, or lack of interest, in religious and ethnic identity per se.

However the descendants of intermarriage affiliate, and even if we are staunchly secular in outlook, unattached to any particular spiritual or ethnic community, our position as isolated observers is probably traceable to the effects of intolerance. A glass curtain of bigotry separates us not only from anti-Semites but from the "born" Jews who fear us. Put bluntly, the fervor with which some Jewish-identified descendants of intermarriage embrace Jewish life can make "born" Jews feel defensive, or worse. They wonder why we care so much. And some members of the Jewish community have confided to us that they suspect that welcoming snub-nosed, Anglo-Saxon–surnamed descendants of intermarriage will mean the end of Judaism as they know it.

But what, precisely, are they afraid of? American Jews who mourn the remnants of *shtetl* (the "Old Country") and Lower East Side culture, who glorify the *bubbes* and *zaydes* whose pious habits were so quickly abandoned by their assimilated children and grandchildren, are living in a dream world. Like Ronald Reagan's apple-cheeked vision of small-town America, this schmaltzy vista of turn-of-the-century *Yiddishkeit* can never be reclaimed—indeed, was never an accurate picture of Jewish life for many Sephardim and other non-Ashkenazic Jews.

American Judaism needs revival, not reverie. There's no better place to start than with the descendants of intermarriage, and no time like the present. If programs addressing our needs are developed—for starters, following a few of the suggestions outlined below—the American Jewish community will grow rapidly and joyfully, with a vigor unparalleled in Diaspora Jewish history.

A grandiose claim? Not at all. If appropriate action is taken by the Jewish community, those descendants of intermarriage who identify as Jews will indeed be *real, willing, active* Jews. Unlike the predominantly secular American Jewish community of today, many of whose members are openly bored by or resentful of their Jewish identity, the descendants of intermarriage who opt to live as Jews will have *freely chosen* to join synagogues, donate to Jewish causes, support Israel (warts and all), learn Hebrew, perform home-based rituals, and enroll their kids in Jewish nurseries, camps, and Hebrew schools.

Our Christian and secular brothers and sisters, positively tied to Judaism through their parentage as well as their Jewish-identified siblings, will join us in our celebrations, grieve with us in times of sorrow, and will continue to care about the fate of the Jewish people. If, God forbid, Jews need Gentile allies in a time of crisis, our extended families will be there for us.

The stark black-and-white picture that is sketched by many doomsayers shows a weary, secular Jewish community that shrinks as its elders die off, and its young people defect to non-Jewish faiths and philosophies. In truth, both the secular *and* the religious Judaism of the future can be as colorful and vibrant as a Chagall window, if *every* Jewish organization makes it a high priority to incorporate the concerns of the descendants of intermarriage into *every* program they sponsor.

The initiatives we suggest below are neither complex nor expensive. They rely upon consciousness-raising that will impress upon every Jew the need for person-to-person, "each one teach one" outreach to the descendants of intermarriage, and upon a broad-based institutional awareness of our legitimate, urgent needs. Specifically incorporating the adult descendants of intermarriage into outreach saves time and energy, as the Jewish community's educational lifeline can then be tossed out to all, reaching disaffected secular Jews and interfaith couples as well. Nobody loses, everybody wins.

Synagogues are usually the first point of contact for descendants of intermarriage who wish to explore their Jewish "halves." In many areas with sparse Jewish populations, a synagogue may be the *only* significant Jewish social resource. Consequently, rabbis, cantors, administrators, educators, sisterhood officers, and others must be aware that they can make a crucial difference in how a descendant of intermarriage feels about his or her Jewishness. Officers of Jewish communal groups should remember this as well, as they may come into contact with descendants of intermarriage who desire to affiliate with a secular or strongly political Jewish group rather than with a house of worship. The initiatives described below are equally applicable to both religious and secular Jewish groups.

• **Start ongoing support groups for the teenage and adult children and grandchildren of Jewish-Gentile intermarriage, as well as for endogamously wed Jews whose offspring have married Gentiles.** Publicize the meeting times and locations in the temple or Jewish community center bulletin as well as in the local Jewish newspaper. Bear in mind that outreach efforts aimed solely at interfaith couples will not suffice—we are not our parents, and our concerns differ markedly from theirs. Promote these groups in all literature aimed at prospective members, as well as in the advertisements typically placed in Jewish newspapers around the High Holidays to recruit new members.

• **Lobby your denominational or organizational headquarters to create new educational materials for teen and adult descendants of intermarriage.** This book is one resource, but we hope that there will be many, many more. Even a simple pamphlet would be helpful.

• **Designate one synagogue staff member, whether paid or volunteer, as the coordinator for the members of interfaith families.** Integrating the descendants of intermarriage and their interfaith parents into religious, educational, and social activities should be this person's primary responsibility. When cold-calling a synagogue, members of interfaith families often feel defensive or hesitant. A sensitive coordinator can do much to allay their fears of rejection.

In addition, at every service and social function, at least one person should be assigned the task of watching for newcomers. Welcome them. Ask them if there's anything they need to know, or what they're most interested in exploring about Jewish life. Offer them informational brochures about the synagogue's membership policies and educational opportunities. Seat them next to a friendly person who can help them find their way through the service, introduce them to others in attendance, and answer any other questions they may have.

• **If synagogue policy does not permit unconverted patrilineal (or even, in some cases, matrilineal) descendants of intermarriage or Gentiles married to Jews to join, consider instituting a two-tier membership system.** Full membership can be offered to those whose Jewish status is not ambiguous. A second category of conditional membership can be made available to the Gentile spouses or other partners of Jewish members and to those who are studying for conversion to Judaism, whether they have one Gentile parent or two. The synagogue might specify, for instance, that whereas it would like to see everyone in the second category progress to full membership eventually, the conditional plan allows them to enjoy the company and services provided by the synagogue without making a premature, uninformed commitment.

• **Consider instituting a flexible dues schedule.** Descendants of intermarriage and unaffiliated "born" Jews alike often hesitate to join synagogues, especially during their unfettered single years, because they fear that it will be too costly. And oftentimes membership is beyond their reach. Granted, it's expensive to maintain a congregation, to pay the rabbi and the electric company and the custodians and the bakery that supplies the pastries for *oneg Shabbat*. And many, if not most, synagogue administrators will adjust membership fees on a case-by-case basis—but only if the newcomer swallows his or her pride to ask.

If synagogues routinely set up sliding-scale fees, adjusted for income and need for *shul* services (families with Hebrew-school–age children would pay more, for example), and established monthly billing plans that spread payment for dues and pledges throughout the year, more people would gladly join without feeling like charity cases. Even if some congregants write much smaller checks than others, adding more members translates into more income for the synagogue, and more actively committed Jews.

• **Improve Jewish outreach.** Paradoxically, centuries of persecution have held Jewish communities together, in part because Jews were tolerated only within their own ghettoes. In pluralistic, democratic nations such as the United States, Canada, and the United Kingdom, it's been difficult for Jewish communities to retain as many of their members as they'd like. *No* religious culture in a free society can count on ethnic bonding alone to retain its members. By an alchemy peculiar to democracies, *any* religious culture that fails to reach out persistently to its members will see some of them siphoned off by other, more aggressively self-confident groups.

• **Improve institutional visibility.** Lawn placards often urge passersby to save Soviet or Ethiopian Jewry. Yet synagogues rarely communicate their concern for the home team by erecting signs that proclaim in large letters, for example, SHABBAT SERVICES, FRIDAYS, 7 P.M. ALL ARE WELCOME! Without such a message, many diffident descendants of intermarriage and their parents, as well as nonaffiliated Jews, might drive right on past, assuming they *wouldn't* be welcome at a strange *shul*. Make your hospitality known.

A fine example of an unusually welcoming message appeared in this recent newspaper ad for Adat Shalom Reconstructionist Congregation of Bethesda, Maryland: "Whatever your background or level of Jewish commitment or knowledge, if you are looking for a synagogue community where you can learn, celebrate, and grow Jewishly, Adat Shalom might be for you."

• **Open your minds and hearts.** Although they may appear wary and cautious, descendants of intermarriage are visiting a synagogue or group because they really want to learn about Judaism. Unlike many secular "born" Jews, they're not likely to just show up out of habit, to please their parents, or because it "looks good." We want to know other Jews' attitudes about God, prayer, ritual, history, and politics. Many descendants of intermarriage long to connect with a community that has a long, proud, battered, and noble history. If we choose Judaism for that reason, we hope that others will help us to affirm that choice.

• **Be patient and nonjudgmental.** Many well-meaning members of synagogues and Jewish organizations are astounded by our polyglot backgrounds ("Your mother was a Jew, and she raised you as a Presbyterian? How could she?"), or by the seemingly obvious aspects of synagogue ritual with which we may be unfamiliar ("We *always* rise when the Ark doors are opened"), or even by the extent of our familiarity with Judaism ("How come you know so much when you're not even a 'real' Jew?").

The descendants of intermarriage who seek to explore our Jewish "halves" hope that "born" Jews will put their astonishment aside and welcome our interest, without making any attempt to shame us for our lack of knowledge, if that's the case, or for our status as an adult child or grandchild of intermarriage. If a particular synagogue or group is not quite the right place for us, we welcome suggestions of others in which we might feel more comfortable. The goal is to keep a Jewish-oriented descendant of intermarriage within Judaism. If we turn to another faith or way of life, it shouldn't be simply because we felt unwelcome within the Jewish community.

• **If you are a rabbi who comes into contact with engaged or married interfaith couples, as well as adult descendants of intermarriage, never underestimate your power to influence their feelings—positive or negative—toward Judaism.** Time and again, our research revealed instances in which the words and deeds of a single rabbi affected several generations of a single family. An interfaith couple's perception of how they are viewed by the Jewish community will color their children's and grandchildren's self-images for many years to come.

This doesn't mean that you have to dish out platitudes to a couple who may hunger for unqualified approval. Just tell them what's at stake in an interfaith marriage. Tell them which branches of Judaism consider their children "real" Jews, which do not, and why. Tell them what's involved in order to change that status. Tell them what their marriage means to the Jewish and Christian worlds in nonjudgmental, everyday, concrete terms. Offer them reading lists, and put them in contact with others who share their status. Tell the interfaith couple what they can do, through their own example, to change certain hidebound attitudes. This all seems so simple, but believe us, it's rare.

Conservative and Orthodox rabbis may not perform intermarriages, and there is a wide range of opinion, pro and con, among Reform and Reconstructionist rabbis as to whether officiating at such a wedding is desirable. If your disapproval, whether personal or denominational, prevents you from officiating or co-officiating, do consider referring the engaged couple to another rabbi or cantor who might agree to perform the marriage (see page 207). It's unlikely that an engaged couple will decide not to marry simply because a particular rabbi said no to them, but the rejection may very well sour them on Judaism in *any* form, and might discourage them from teaching their children anything positive about their Jewish "half." And *that* is to be avoided.

In improving dialogue with the members of interfaith families, the immediate goal is to persuade them to come out of hiding, acknowledge their differences, and celebrate them where possible. Thus emboldened, some will affiliate Jewishly, and others will not. But the long-term mission of the Jewish community should be to ensure that *all* descendants of intermarriage love the part of themselves that is Jewish, *however* they choose to identify. Historically, we have not been encouraged to do so, and now the future of Diaspora Judaism depends upon it.

We'll end this book where all descendants of intermarriage begin, among the families who gave us life. While we've already offered many suggestions to interfaith parents in previous chapters, our extended families also can play a special role in our adult lives. Grandparents and other relatives often ask how they can help us achieve a greater understanding of one of our "halves." When we're small, some grandparents ferociously promote their own way of life, especially if we're being raised in a culture different from theirs. Others fear above all being perceived as pushy or preachy, so these good souls back off altogether, murmuring, "I don't want your parents to think I'm interfering."

Once we're adults, free to choose, free to explore, we can reassure our relatives that between these two extremes is a desirable middle ground where we can meet.

• **Be there for us.** Many descendants of intermarriage mourn the loss of relatives who have fallen out of touch because they disagreed with their interfaith parents' religious and cultural choices. Uncles and aunts, grandparents and cousins who send us cards and presents at the appropriate holidays, who invite us to their *seders* and Easter-egg hunts, and who make it clear that we are part of their family no matter how we affiliate fill a deep need of ours in a truly positive manner.

• **Tell us about our roots.** If we weren't raised scrupulously as "real" Jews or "real" Christians, grandparents especially are likely to worry that a random anecdote or invitation, casually offered, would be essentially meaningless in the grand scheme of things. Not so! If Rabbi Nachman of Bratislav were still alive, he'd tell these hesitant relatives that even the smallest gesture toward the good causes great changes in the upper worlds. And many descendants of intermarriage have spoken movingly of how participating in a single event—a family gathering, a class—has motivated them to grow closer to one of their birth cultures, or even to make dramatic changes in their religious and cultural affiliation.

Our interfaith parents, afraid to open a Pandora's box of identity questions from their children, may offer only the sketchiest of details about the two families' backgrounds. Here's where our grandparents and other relatives can step in to tell us more. This can give us more grounding upon which to choose one parental culture over another. At the very least, we'll enjoy a newfound pride and understanding.

• **Support our choices.** Knowing that we have sympathetic relatives to turn to is especially reassuring for the descendants of intermarriage who affiliate with a faith or culture different from the one in which we were raised, especially if our interfaith parents and/or siblings disapprove or don't care. Grandparents, cousins, in-laws, and others can help to heal some of the isolation and grief we may feel at journeying down a road that may take us away from the rest of our family.

Fortunately, isolation and grief are only part of the story of the descendants of Jewish-Gentile intermarriage—a very small part, for some of us. By the circumstances of our birth, we're obliged to embark on what may be a long, arduous journey, during which we learn to juggle our dual religious and ethnic heritages. We must learn how to honor the conflicting demands of our "two halves" and still maintain our balance.

However rocky the road, our quest for an integrated identity allows us to fully develop positive and wondrous qualities that we didn't even know we possessed. Being forced to determine for ourselves who we are, and what beliefs fit us best, makes us strong yet flexible, self-reliant as well as receptive to others, humorous yet serious, tolerant and decisive. When our anger is transformed into energy, we are capable of amazing growth and action. When our energy is expressed through love, we influence others by our example. We pledge allegiance to at least two worlds, and often feel a deeply moving kinship with many more. This is what being a descendant of Jewish-Gentile intermarriage is all about.

Glossary of Hebrew and Yiddish Terms

aliyah The honor of being called before a Jewish congregation to recite the blessings that precede and follow a reading from the Torah.

ba'al teshuvah "One who has returned." A term applied to a secular Jew who becomes observant.

bet din "House of justice." A panel of three rabbis who arbitrate complaints that Jews bring against one another, and who also determine whether a prospective convert is sincere and should be admitted to the Jewish people.

brachot (sing., *bracha*) Blessings and benedictions.

bris Ritual circumcision for Jewish males, generally performed on the eighth day of life, or before conversion.

bubbe Yiddish term for "grandmother."

Chabad House Located in cities around the world, Chabad houses are staffed by members of the Lubavitcher Hasidim, an Orthodox Jewish group that devotes much energy outreaching to unaffiliated and nonobservant Jews. Chabad houses provide a setting for classes, religious services, and social activities for Lubavitcher and other Jews.

daven Phrase meaning "to pray." *Davening* generally applies to praying in Hebrew.

ger Convert to Judaism.

goy (pl., *goyim*) Non-Jew.

halacha Jewish law.

havurah A group, generally small and informal, that meets for Jewish worship and socializing. *Havurot* (pl.) may exist as independent entities or as part of a synagogue.

kashrut The Jewish dietary laws, which call for strict separation of meat and milk products, certain methods of food preparation, rabbinic supervision of processed and restaurant foods, and prohibit the consumption of pork and shellfish.

kavannah Intent and concentration in prayer and in the performance of Jewish rituals.

kipah Skullcap (also known by its Yiddish name, *yarmulke*) worn in synagogue by Jewish males (and some females), and during all waking hours by observant Jewish men and boys.

k'lal Yisrael The community of Israel.

kohen A Jew who enjoys priestly status. Certain honors are granted to a *kohen* (such as the first *aliyah* in the Torah reading), and there are certain prohibitions on activity, such as that a *kohen* may never enter a cemetery unless a member of his immediate family is being interred.

levi   A Jew who enjoys secondary, levitical status. A Jew who is neither a *kohen* nor a *levi* is known as an Israelite.

menorah   Candelabrum, found in synagogues and Jewish homes. The Hanukkah *menorah* has nine branches, holding one candle for each of the eight nights of the holiday, plus the *shammas*—the "helper candle"—used to light the others.

mikveh   Ritual bath in which observant Jewish women immerse themselves monthly after menstruation. Some observant Jewish men visit the *mikveh* before holidays. For Jews-by-choice, all who convert to Judaism under Orthodox and Conservative ritual will immerse themselves in the *mikveh*, as will many who convert under Reform and Reconstructionist auspices.

mitzvah (pl. *mitzvot*)   A commandment from the Torah or rabbinic tradition. Also a popular phrase for a good deed.

mohel   Ritual circumcisor.

neshama   Soul.

oneg Shabbat   "Pleasure of the Sabbath." Coffee-and-chatter gatherings held after *Shabbat* services.

Pareveh   A variant Yiddish spelling of the Hebrew word *pareve*, which denotes foods that are neither meat nor milk, but can be served with either. When naming the group for adult children of intermarriage that they co-founded, the authors chose Pareveh as a humorous summary of the situation in which the children of intermarriage find themselves. As this book demonstrates, we truly can go "either way"—and do.

Pirke Avot   Known as "Ethics of the Fathers," this section of the Talmud contains many aphorisms and ethical standards, which are frequently studied on *Shabbat.*

seder   Traditional Passover dinner.

Shabbat   The Jewish Sabbath, which begins before sundown on Friday night and ends one hour after sundown on Saturday. Also known as *Shabbos,* a word used as a noun or adjective (as in "Shabbos candles").

shaygetz (pl., *shkotzim*)   Pejorative term for a Gentile male or males.

shiksa   Uncomplimentary word for a Gentile female.

shivah   The first seven days of mourning observed for a deceased Jewish relative.

shomer shabbos   Sabbath-observant.

shul   Another name for synagogue.

shtetl   Small Eastern European villages in which Jews clustered before the great wave of immigration to the United States and other countries in the late nineteenth and early twentieth centuries.

siddur   Jewish prayer book.

taharas hamishpachah   The laws of ritual purity observed by traditional Jewish husbands and wives, involving sexual separation during menstruation and seven days thereafter, culminating in the wife's visit to the *mikveh*.

tallis   Prayer shawl worn by males (and some females) during morning prayers.

trup   The cantillations that govern how the Torah and Haftorah portions will be read (or "sung") in synagogue.

tuchus   Yiddish term for one's buttocks.

yiches   Jewish lineage.

zayde   Yiddish term for "grandfather."

Resources

Books of Interest to Grown Children
of Jewish-Gentile Intermarriage

Berman, Louis A., *Jews and Intermarriage: A Study in Personality and Culture* (New York: Thos. Yoseloff, 1968).

Cowan, Paul, with Rachel Cowan, *Mixed Blessings: Marriage Between Jews and Christians* (New York: Doubleday, 1987).

Gruzen, Lee F., *Raising Your Jewish/Christian Child: How Interfaith Parents Can Give Children the Best of Both Their Heritages* (New York: Newmarket Press, 1990).

Jacobs, Rabbi Sidney J., and Betty J. Jacobs, *122 Clues for Jews Whose Children Intermarry* (Culver City, California: Jacobs Ladder Publications, 1988). To obtain a copy, send $9.95 plus $1.50 shipping and handling (California residents, add 6.75% tax) to Jacobs Ladder Publications, P.O. Box 1484, Culver City, CA 90232.

Mayer, Egon, *Children of Intermarriage: A Study in Patterns of Identification and Jewish Life* (New York: The American Jewish Committee, 1983).

———, *Love and Tradition: Marriage Between Jews and Christians* (New York and London: Plenum Press, 1985).

Mayer, John E., *Jewish-Gentile Courtships: An Exploratory Study of a Social Process* (New York: The Free Press of Glencoe, Inc., 1961).

Packouz, Rabbi Kalman, *How to Stop an Intermarriage* (Spring Valley, New York: Philipp Feldheim Inc., 1976).

Petsonk, Judy, and Jim Remsen, *The Intermarriage Handbook: A Guide for Jews and Christians* (New York: Arbor House/William Morrow and Company, Inc., 1988).

Portnoy, Rabbi Mindy Avra, *Mommy Never Went to Hebrew School* (Rockville, Maryland: Kar-Ben Copies, Inc., 1989).

Reuben, Rabbi Steven Carr, *But How Will You Raise the Children?: A Guide to Interfaith Marriage* (New York: Pocket Books, 1987).

Roiphe, Anne, *Generation Without Memory: A Jewish Journey in Christian America* (New York: The Linden Press/Simon & Schuster, 1981).

Rosenberg, Rabbi Roy A., Father Peter Meehan, and the Reverend John Wade Payne, *Happily Intermarried: Authoritative Advice for a Joyous Jewish-Christian Marriage* (New York: Macmillan, 1988).

Schneider, Susan Weidman, *Intermarriage: The Challenge of Living with the Differences Between Christians and Jews* (New York: The Free Press, 1989).

Seltzer, Rabbi Sanford, *Jews and Non-Jews: Getting Married* (New York: Union of American Hebrew Congregations, 1984).

Selected Resources for Members of Interfaith Families

Al-Anon Family Group Headquarters, Inc.
P.O. Box 862
Midtown Station
New York, NY 10018-0862
(212) 302-7240

Concerned United Birthparents, Inc., is a national, nonprofit organization "dedicated to providing mutual help to all adoption-affected persons," including birth parents, adoptees, adoptive parents, and others. It maintains a "reunion registry" for birth parents and children, publishes a wide variety of material about adoption issues, and offers support to those in need. For more information, write or call CUB, Inc., 2000 Walker Street, Des Moines, IA 50317, (515) 263-9558, or call toll-free (800) 822-2777.

The Interracial Family Circle's goal is "communicating information, ideas, and concerns to all who support a family of more than one race." The IFC sponsors activities for interracial and intercultural individuals and families. Membership dues are $25 for the first year and $20 per year thereafter, and a monthly newsletter is provided. For more information, write the IFC, P.O. Box 53290, Washington, D.C. 20009.

Jewish Ties calls itself "the independent newsletter for interfaith couples, Jews by choice, Jews by birth, and their families." Addressing a wide variety of provocative and pertinent topics, *Jewish Ties* is available for $18 per year (six issues); back issues are $3.50 apiece. For more information, write or call Lewis Copulsky, Lewis & Clark Associates, 6508 Valley Estates Drive, P.O. Box 31027, Raleigh, NC 27622-1027, (919) 676-2036.

Looking Up, a support group for incest survivors, protects anonymity and will tailor the services it provides according to individual needs. For more information, write or call Looking Up, P.O. Box K, Augusta, ME 04330, (207) 626-3402.

National Tay-Sachs and Allied Diseases, Inc.
2001 Beacon Street
Suite 304
Brookline, MA 02146
(617) 277-4463

Pareveh, The Alliance for the Adult Children of Jewish-Gentile Intermarriage, founded in 1985 by the authors of this book, offers a tape library, speakers, and advice of interest to the adult descendants of intermarriage, interfaith couples, and the parents of interfaith couples. A lengthy bibliography—too long to include in this book!—of articles and books is also available. For more information, write or call Pareveh, 3628 Windom Place, N.W., Washington, D.C. 20008, (202) 828-3020.

The Rabbinic Center for Research and Counseling provides psychological and spiritual outreach services to interfaith couples. Affiliated with the "experimental, experiential" Rabbinic Center Synagogue, the organization maintains a national listing, updated every other month, of members of the Central Conference of American Rabbis (Reform) and the Reconstructionist Rabbinical Association who will officiate at intermarriages under certain specified conditions. For more information, write or call the Rabbinic Center for Research and Counseling, 128 East Dudley Avenue, Westfield, NJ 07090, (201) 233-0419. To obtain a copy of the list, which costs $15, call (908) 233-2288.

Stars of David International, Inc., calls itself "the quintessential nonprofit information/support/social network for Jewish and partly Jewish families" who are raising their adoptive children as Jews, but with an appreciation for their birth cultures as well. (It is not an adoption agency.) Membership is $8 per year in the United States, $11 per year elsewhere, and includes their periodic newsletter, "Star Tracks." For more information, write Janie Allen, 9 Hampton Street, Cranford, NJ 07016, or Lisa Jackson, 5231 E. Memorial Drive #175, Stone Mountain, GA 30083.

About the Authors

LESLIE GOODMAN-MALAMUTH graduated from the School of Journalism at the University of California at Berkeley. She is a freelance writer and a former staff editor at *Legal Times, Nutrition Action Health Letter, California Lawyer,* and *Sierra, The Sierra Club Bulletin.* Leslie lives with her husband and sons in Washington, D.C.

ROBIN MARGOLIS holds a bachelor's degree in biology and a master's in counseling from the University of Virginia. Formerly a law librarian and paralegal, she is currently the editor of *HealthSpan,* a health care law and public policy magazine published by Prentice Hall Law & Business. Robin lives in Washington, D.C.